Garden Ponds

Garden Ponds

10 step-by-step projects

Quick and easy ideas to enhance your garden

Bryan Hirst

NEW HOLLAND

First published in 2004 by New Holland Publishers (UK) Ltd
London • Cape Town • Sydney • Auckland

Garfield House, 86–88 Edgware Road, London W2 2EA, United Kingdom
www.newhollandpublishers.com

80 McKenzie Street, Cape Town 8001, South Africa

Level 1, Unit 4, 14 Aquatic Drive, Frenchs Forest, NSW 2086, Australia

218 Lake Road, Northcote, Auckland

ISBN 1 84330 128 8

2 4 6 8 10 9 7 5 3 1

Editorial Direction: Rosemary Wilkinson
Project Editor: Clare Sayer
Production: Hazel Kirkman
Editor: Ian Keary

Project design (p 37, 53, 71 and 83): AG&G Books and Bryan Hirst
Project construction (p 37, 53, 71 and 83): AG&G Books
Planting and props (p 37, 53, 71 and 83): AG&G Books, Vana Haggerty and John Heming
Photography: John Freeman, AG&G Books and Ian Parsons
Illustrator: Gill Bridgewater   Designer: Glyn Bridgewater

Reproduction by Pica Digital Pte Ltd, Singapore
Printed and bound in Malaysia by Times Offset (M) Sdn. Bhd.

Conversion chart

To convert the metric measurements given in this book to imperial measurements, simply multiply the figure given in the text by the relevant number shown in the table alongside. Bear in mind that conversions will not necessarily work out exactly, and you will need to round the figure up or down slightly. (Do not use a combination of metric and imperial measurements – for accuracy, keep to one system.)

To convert	Multiply by
millimetres to inches	0.0394
metres to feet	3.28
metres to yards	1.093
sq millimetres to sq inches	0.00155
sq metres to sq feet	10.76
sq metres to sq yards	1.195
cu metres to cu feet	35.31
cu metres to cu yards	1.308
grams to pounds	0.0022
kilograms to pounds	2.2046
litres to gallons	0.22

Contents

Natural pond
36

Planted stream
42

Kidney-shaped
pond
46

Circular pond
52

Formal canal
58

Pond with bridge
and beach
64

Raised pond
70

Pond with decking
76

Mosaic pond
82

Split-level pool
88

Introduction

Over the last ten years I have spent much of my time studying, building and improving ponds and water features. The knowledge that I have gained will, I hope, give you the confidence to build your own uniquely beautiful water feature which will give you and generations to come endless pleasure and delight.

Because of modern technology it is now relatively easy and inexpensive to build a pond in your garden. This book outlines the principles and practices of building, planting and maintaining ponds which use flexible liners and modern materials, or traditional methods where appropriate, and is full of useful information.

This beautiful pond is the focal point in a classic garden. It requires careful planning and construction but is worth the effort (see page 58).

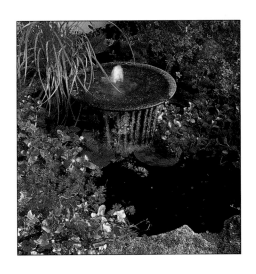

Once you have grasped the principles, there is no limit to what your location, imagination and hard work can achieve when it comes to building a pond in your garden. There are ten very different ponds in this book, ranging from informal, natural ponds to raised brick ones.

The music of falling water adds to the serenity and beauty of a garden pond. Many designs have room for a fountain or small water feature.

Water has a special significance in our lives. Apart from the fact that our bodies and souls need it to function properly, it has a calming and soothing influence. A pond at the heart of the garden is a captivating element – water and light can enchant the eye and lift the spirit. The achievement of true contentment is difficult at best and impossible without water. The importance of water, for me, was exemplified in the garden during an Indian summer evening. My daughter was mesmerised by the water skaters dancing between the lilies on the surface of the water, my partner was drinking a glass of wine listening to the waterfall, I saw the plants and the sky reflected on the water and looking deeper saw the fronds of the submerged plants teeming with life. All was well in the world that I shared and had helped to create. Perhaps the same delights await you.

Bryan R Klint.

Health and safety

If you are thoughtful and take care when working, any potential hazards are easily avoided. Before starting work, consider the following:

✔ Is it safe to build a pond in your garden if you have young children? (See page 13?)

✔ For some pond building procedures you will need to wear gloves, goggles and a dust mask and take some basic precautions. (See pages 20 and 22.)

✔ Make sure that you are strong and fit enough for the task ahead.

✔ Immobilise any equipment or lock it up and make sure that a safety barrier or tape stops anyone wandering unprepared into your excavation.

✔ Have a first-aid kit and telephone within easy reach. If possible, avoid working alone.

Part 1
Techniques

Designing and planning

Building a water feature is a big undertaking that involves a fair amount of hard work and as it is designed to be a permanent feature of the garden, planning is essential. The decisions to be made are based partly on what sort of pond you want, and partly on the limitations of your garden. These and the following pages suggest pond types, locations and functions to help you choose what suits your needs best.

Types of pond

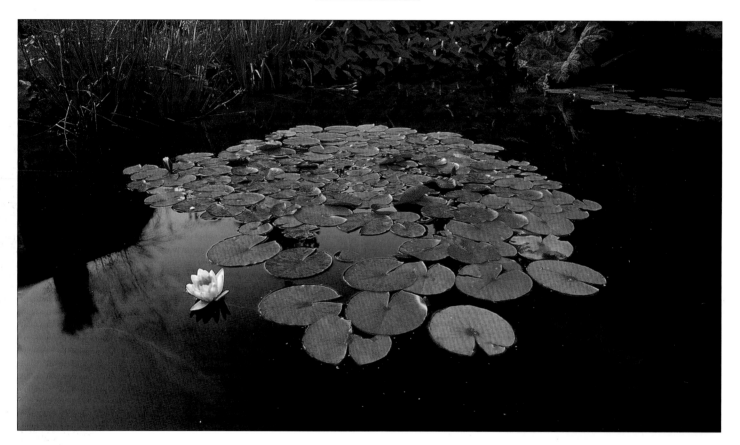

Natural pond

This pond follows the forms and curves of nature, with no built-up edges, and perhaps includes an outcrop of stone or a beach. This allows for planting, where appropriate, in and at the edges of the pond and gives the impression that the water was there long before the rest of the garden and house were constructed.

Bog garden

Wet areas, often located next to ponds, support a wide range of plants that do not grow in ordinary garden conditions. Bog gardens can be built to stand alone or as part of an informal pond.

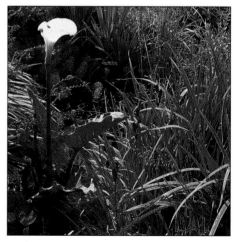

Above: For a natural-looking pond to be completely successful, the lining must be entirely hidden from view, especially at the edges. Restrained planting suitable for a natural pond is also a key feature.
Right: Include a boggy area in your pond design if you want to grow plants like this Arum lily, one of a large range of plants that will thrive with roots under water.

Above: As well as offering the delights of water lilies which will flower all summer long, this sunken formal brick pond brings the sky down to earth with constantly changing reflections and leads the eye down the full length of the pond.

Formal pond

A geometric design works best if it forms an association in materials and design with the buildings that are close to it. It may, for example, be rectangular, octagonal or linear in form, and may have a stone or paved edge that allows easy access to the water's edge. Where possible, any change of level can be exploited with small waterfalls running from the higher to the lower pond. Planting is possible in a formal pond, although this is more likely to be a few carefully chosen architectural plants, rather than a large number.

Raised pond

This is a formal pond constructed above ground level and contained by brick or stone walls. Its advantage is that it reduces the amount of spoil that needs to be removed from the site; however, this saving is usually absorbed by the increased cost of construction of the exterior walls. As they will be a major feature, they often require finishing materials that can be more expensive than hidden construction materials, where the finish is not important.

Above: If a raised pond is at a comfortable sitting height (450 mm is ideal), it is fascinating to dabble or to watch the varied life in the pond life close up whilst enjoying a drink or contemplating life.

Rill or stream

The principles of creating a stream or a rill are more or less the same. A stream is designed to appear entirely natural, whereas a rill, or channel, is a formally contained stream. You can use a slope by creating an apparently natural source of water: this is achieved by pumping water to a disguised source, giving the impression of water coming up from a spring. The character of the stream or rill will be altered by the gradient of the ground. The steeper the gradient, the greater the potential for pools and waterfalls.

This gentle stream with planting along the edges allows you to make the most of a slight gradient. If your garden is steep enough, you can have waterfalls as the water makes its way down. The stream must nestle comfortably in the ground for it to look natural.

Locations

Marking the shape

When you have worked out all the possible locations for your pond, mark them out with lengths of rope or a garden hose, or even spray paint. Marking out the pond shape and viewing it from all aspects allows you to be sure that the end shape (which is difficult and expensive to change) is exactly what you expected. If you have the technology, it is worth photographing the area with a digital camera and manipulating the image to see how this can affect reality. Should any trees be reshaped, reduced or removed? Are there any natural dips or gullies that could be made to hold water, or any slopes from which water could run from fountain to pond? Is there a vista that you can reflect in the surface of your pond?

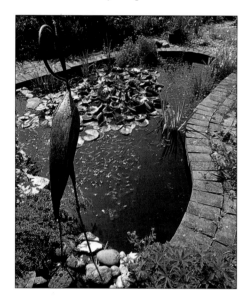

Above: The natural lie of the land will dictate the shape and character of a pond. Gentle curves are easier on the eye than sharp bends in informal settings. Nature abhors straight lines and perfect circles. Above right: This natural looking pond makes the most of its beautiful setting, allowing the reflections of the sky to reach up to the edge of the pond and tempting you down to the water's edge. The grassy bank edging the pond is perfect for sitting by the water on summer days.

Natural advantages

The surface of a pond reflects light and all the changing humours of the weather and seasons, and the placing of what is effectively a mirror surface to gain the most from this quality is something that should be given major consideration. Studying the movement of the sun across the horizon may give you an opportunity to create a dappled effect on the ceiling or walls inside your house, and to bring more light into a shady area. Place mirrors in the intended pond area to help evaluate the effect of the reflected light.

Visibility

To get the most from your pond it is often best to site it where you can see it from inside your house – perhaps from your bedroom window or the kitchen or recreation areas – so you can enjoy its appearance changing with the time of day as well as the seasons. Remember that the perceived shape of the pond will be altered by the viewpoint: for example, an oval pond will appear round when viewed along the greater length, as the apparent length will become reduced.

Alternatively, some of the most exciting ponds are sited away from a property and require a walk to them. If your garden is large enough, try to have some part of the pond not immediately visible from the house, as this encourages the adventure of a search and exploration of the grounds to reveal the whole picture.

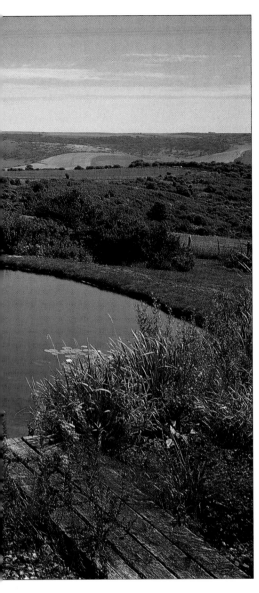

Child safety

Children can and sometimes do get into trouble in ponds, and it is important to consider all potential hazards. A raised pond deters children from crawling or stumbling into it, or borders can be built around the inside perimeter of the pond to keep children out of water that is more than 75 mm deep. A custom-made decorative steel grid could be used.

The design of some fountains allows stones to be placed in the basin to reduce the depth of the water; these can be removed later when children have reached a safer age. Another alternative is to delay the project until your children have reached an age when they do not need constant supervision near water.

Make sure that it is not possible to drive a car or other machinery into the water – for example, if the pond is to be near car parking areas or driveways, put up bollards, posts or raised kerbs to physically stop any runaway machines.

Ease of use

Make sure that you can approach the pond easily and that there is going to be provision for seating near the pond on a flat surface. Consider placing a pergola, barbecue or dining area near the pond.

Stepping stones sunk into a lawn will allow you to approach the pond during the winter or when the grass is wet. Make sure that the stones are well set into the ground and will not interfere with the mowing. People naturally congregate by a pond so make enough space by it.

By-products

If your pond is to be dug out, rather than raised, consider what are you going to do with the excavated material (spoil). Can you build up a bank, or should you take the spoil away, which can be expensive and difficult? If you are removing good topsoil, look at possible uses elsewhere to add to the quality of the soil, or to level another section of your property. It is easy to underestimate the amount that you will have to take away – often it bulks up and becomes up to a third more in volume than when it was in the ground.

Neighbours

If your project can be seen or heard by the neighbours, check that they have no objection to your proposed scheme. A rock waterfall, for example, will be heard by your neighbours and may cause them irritation. Excavations can affect the foundations of a neighbour's house or outhouses, fences or trees, as well as the water table or water supply to adjoining properties. If you consider that any of these factors could be a problem, consult an engineer.

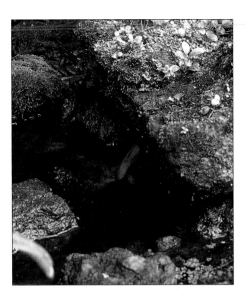

Experiment with sound by adjusting the volume of water flowing over waterfalls and by positioning stones to alter the music.

Sound

For many, the sound of running water from a stream or fountain gives an enormous sense of calm and relaxation. This sound may be tuned or adjusted by altering the volume of water that is flowing, or by placing obstacles, such as stones or rocks, in the path of the water.

Obstacles checklist

✔ Are there underground services, which may be affected by your workings? Check with the relevant utilities companies.

✔ Consider the type of soil and what lies underneath it: for example, solid rock will be expensive to break up and remove, clay soil requires hard work to dig deeply and it is impossible to make clean-sided holes in sandy soil.

✔ Could there be the foundations of an earlier building or construction?

✔ Are there any large plants or trees nearby which are likely to have wide spreading roots that you need to avoid cutting through?

✔ Has the ground been disturbed and polluted or made unstable?

Functions

The next consideration is what you want the water feature to do for you, and how important each of your requirements is, compared to each other.

Reflections

Watching still waters reflect the changing weather patterns in the sky can be immensely enjoyable, and these reflections are radically altered if water from a fountain falls on to the surface of the pond. A waterfall will ripple the surface and break up light reflections.

Falling water is fascinating; it catches the sunlight as well as causing ripples and breaking up the surface of the pool below.

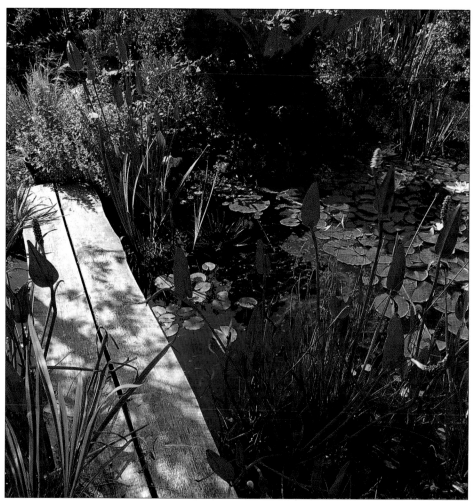

As a natural pond matures, the surface of the water will be covered with plants. Arrange in groups or stands of the same plants together as the effect is generally more pleasing and the area is easier to maintain. Below: Wildlife will come naturally to your pond. Attempts to import wildlife are unsuccessful as each habitat will support particular life.

Entertainment

Waterside entertainment has some added magical properties: decking allows you to be over the water whilst eating or relaxing; lights placed near the pond reflect in the water to add to the waterside effect; and a barbecue and dining area close to the pond could be considered.

Activity

The scale of your pond may allow boating, fishing, diving and swimming, while even sitting on the edge with your feet in the water on a hot day can give real pleasure. Children may be able to play with model boats. In the evening, floating paper boats with candles in them on the water adds charm and a sense of calm.

Plants

The quality and range of plants that can be grown in and beside the pond affect its visual characteristics enormously. Plants can be positioned in or beside the pond, either in the ground or in suitable containers.

Wildlife

This should come naturally to a pond, although it is possible to encourage certain types of wildlife, such as frogs and newts, by building a beach to allow ease of access. The size and depth of a pond will dictate the range and quantity of the wildlife that use it.

Fish

When a pond has had a year to develop, it can support a small number of fish without upsetting the delicate ecological balance. If, however, you want to keep a considerable number of ornamental fish, you will need to fit filtration and cleaning facilities. These vary in size and type, but be aware that some filtration units can take up an area of up to half the surface area of the pond. Power supplies are required and special pipework needs to be built into the pond; protection for plants must also be installed.

Birds

Ornamental ducks can become tame, and wild birds will often attempt to colonize a pond. If ornamental ducks are planned for your pond, you should build a floating island house where they can be safe from foxes and other vermin; a pebble beach should also be built where they will be encouraged to enter and leave the water, and set up an area where they can rest and be fed. This will also minimize and contain the damage that ducks can do to the surrounding flora.

Filtration should be considered to remove the added nutrients that birds add to the pond through their droppings. These nutrients encourage algae and weeds such as duckweed which can quickly make a pond unsightly.

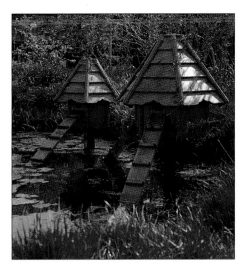

These houses protect birds from vermin such as foxes. They are ideally placed on an island which saves you the daily task of penning and releasing your birds, as most vermin will not swim to attack ducks.

Birds can have a devastating effect on a newly established pond, as they damage young plants. If they are unwelcome, early discouragement before they start nesting should generally be effective. Herons also pose a threat to fish keepers as they will often come at first light and take fish from a pond. There are various ways to discourage them which may be used with varying success. Decoys are available as wrought iron structures that resemble herons but they are often ineffective as the real herons will notice the lack of movement and disregard them after some time. Netting is effective, if unsightly but there are some attractive metal grille options available. Herons like shallow water so a depth of water at the sides of the pond will also deter them.

Practicalities

With the basic design and planning in hand, the next move is to consider the wider effects of adding a pond to your garden – whether it would affect nearby property, for example. Consider your neighbours, talk over your plans and agree the scheme before you start work.

Costs

Undertaking a project yourself is unquestionably the most cost-effective method, as long as you have researched and designed your project well, as most of the cost of building a pond is taken up by moving materials. Costs are hugely affected by access and the difficulties of materials handling, and by hidden factors, which may only be revealed during the excavation. Labour costs can be difficult to estimate, but materials, plant hire and fuel can be more easily estimated and priced. The more you know and are able to do yourself, the lower your costs. Check your bank account before starting, as there is nothing more depressing and morale-lowering than a half-complete project awaiting funds and energy.

Disruption

Unlike interior projects, the weather and amount of rainfall during a pond project can cause problems and increase the time taken to complete it. You know the weather in your area best – however, I do not recommend the undertaking of a project if you are likely to experience frozen ground conditions, heavy rain or intense heat during the work.

Careful routing and storage of building materials minimizes disruption to your household during the works. Earth, concrete and general debris have an uncanny ability to spread themselves over the house, car, driveway, clothes and machinery, and neighbours may complain if machinery is used or work is undertaken during unsociable hours.

Removal of excess materials

A skip container or storage site, easily accessible from the road, may be required. Make sure that the relevant authorities have been informed of your plans and have given any necessary approval. Because trucks may need to

unload materials, make sure that an out-of-the-way location is clearly signposted.

Works access

This may require the co-operation of neighbours and the removal of plants or fence panels, so plan carefully. The narrowest comfortable width for a wheelbarrow to pass through is 1 m; avoid sharp turns where possible, and prepare steps with wooden planks to enable loaded barrows to pass easily over them.

If you are thinking of using an excavator (see page 22), check the minimum width and height required. Note that an excavator needs additional turning space at the sides and it may damage the surface on which it skews, so protect any vulnerable surfaces with boards.

Supply of services

During construction you will need water and electricity. If the project is large, arrange a temporary supply to the key locations using extension cable and hose pipes, so that these services are not affected during the workings.

Pond liners

Until the modern development of manufactured flexible liners, ponds were lined in traditional ways and it is worth considering the possible advantages of using such materials for both aesthetic and practical reasons before making a choice for your project. Availability of materials and costs for additional work in using them can be offset against savings made in the purchase of a modern liner.

Non-flexible liners

Clay

For many years clay was the lining material used for ponds, lakes and waterways; the canals of Great Britain, for example, were mostly made waterproof with puddled clay. In some instances it is still the most cost-effective and best way to line ponds, especially where it is present in the subsoil and there is a plentiful water supply. That said, it has its limitations, as all clay ponds leak to a greater or lesser extent. This may be caused by plants, which put their roots through the clay lining, leaving fissures when the organic materials in the roots rot. It may be also caused by drought: if the water level drops the clay cracks, and when the level rises again water escapes through the cracks and erodes into channels.

Another possibility is that the clay has been mixed with some other unsuitable material that allows water to leach out. To minimize this, clay should be carefully compacted in layers. This is generally done with the tracks of excavators while the clay is still damp. In addition, it is difficult to raise the water level of a clay pond above its natural level, dictated by the surrounding land and water table.

Lead

This material is rarely used in practical ponds today, and water from a lead-lined container should not be drunk. It is, however, supremely long-lasting, as demonstrated by the Roman baths at

Before applying concrete, line the pond with geotextile and butyl

Use a plywood profile to spread and shape the concrete

Once covered with concrete, the liner will remain stable and waterproof for years

Concrete makes the ideal surface for covering with tiles or a mosaic. Before the concrete is applied, the pond should be lined with layers of geotextile and butyl (see opposite).

Bath, England which were made with a 19 mm layer of lead, dressed with stone – there is no record of this ever leaking. Lead is now available in rolls for roof work and can be used, when appropriate, to cover vulnerable or unattractive materials at the water's edge. After a few years it takes on a stable, mellow and attractive finish.

Steel

This is little used, but may have appeal if you are near a shipbuilding centre, where it is readily available. It can be used to create attractive curves and natural shapes, and if good-quality steel is used and the pond is kept full of water, it should have an extended life.

Concrete

Until the arrival of butyl and other flexible membranes, concrete was the favoured material for the building of most garden ponds. It is rarely used today, as it is expensive and has a tendency to crack after some years and leak. When using concrete, it is important to reinforce it with a skeleton of steel and to ensure that the concrete is well prepared and vibrated to make sure that no air gaps are left in the fabric. Specialist contractors undertake this type of work. It is possible to repair concrete ponds under some circumstances, but the repairs are often unsatisfactory and difficult to make permanent.

Fibreglass

Using the same technology as that employed to make boats and certain car bodies, fibreglass can be an attractive option for small ponds where the shape and size are difficult to construct using a flexible liner. The material can also be dyed to any colour required. It is important that sufficient layers of fibreglass are laid down, and that the final gel coat is waterproof. Using fibreglass is an expensive option and is best undertaken by a specialist firm or experienced craftsman.

When fitting a premoulded liner make sure that the voids underneath are carefully filled with sand. Back-fill around the pond, checking the levels as you go.

Preformed pond liners

These come in different shapes and qualities and are best used in very small-scale ponds where the shape is ideal for your purpose – which is rarely the case. When these are used it is important that there are no voids left between the liner and the sand in which it is buried, as these voids lead to stresses which can make the liner crack and leak. Large, irregularly shaped units with different depth zones are difficult to support properly and are more likely to fracture.

Flexible liners

Butyl

Flexible liners have made a huge difference to pond construction. One of the first flexible liners and still the best is butyl rubber, which is used for a wide range of applications, from car windscreen sealant to tyres, each made to a different formulation, principally using petroleum products. Butyl for pond liners is rather like the inner tubes of bicycle tyres in appearance and characteristics, and while it is extremely flexible and stretches without breaking, it is very vulnerable to piercing with sharp objects (again like bicycle tyres). Butyl, therefore, needs to be protected from objects such as flints, sharp stones or gardener's forks. It can, however, be repaired if punctured by cleaning carefully and fitting with a butyl rubber patch. Although it has a very long life, it can be damaged if exposed to ultraviolet light and should be protected with geotextile at all times, especially during construction.

PVC and other flexible liners

These liners are slightly cheaper than butyl, but they share its vulnerability and have none of the benefits of flexibility and reparability. They tend to become brittle in a very few years, and rarely give a satisfactory long-term lining.

Geotextiles

These blanket-like materials – which are not waterproof – are used to stop flexible liners being penetrated by sharp stones and the like. Old carpet or underlay, if non-organic and non-rotting, can be used for the same purpose when savings have to be made. Geotextile is available in various strengths, which are indicated by the weight of material per square metre. Generally, the greater the weight, the stronger and safer the product.

Put just enough water in to hold the liner stable

Do not walk on the liner unless you remove your shoes

Pull the liner up the sides and arrange any folds neatly

After you have positioned the butyl liner, pour some water into the bottom as this will help in neatly arranging any folds or tucks. Adjust any folds as necessary as the water level rises. The pond can be left for a day or two to allow for further settling.

Lay the underlay smoothly. Duct tape can be used to join the underlay and hold it in position while the liner is fitted.

17

Pumps, pipework and lighting

Pumps are used for fountains, streams and waterfalls and may be powered by solar- or mains-generated electricity. Part of the challenge when designing and building a pond is working out how to conceal and protect the electricity supply and water delivery pipes. Remember that water and electricity are a lethal combination. If you are in any doubt about fitting a pump or light, consult a professional.

Submersible electric pumps

These are ideal for most garden pond applications. Silent and invisible when placed at the bottom of a pond or in a balancing chamber, they comprise a sealed electric motor, generally run at mains voltages, and an impeller in a single casing. There are a large number available on the market, of all sizes.

Factors to be considered in choosing submersible pumps are:

✔ The length of the guarantee, now often three years or more.
✔ The effectiveness of the anti-clogging filtration system supplied. Generally, the larger the surface from which the water for the pump is drawn, the less quickly it will become clogged up.
✔ The volume of water pumped and the height to which it can be supplied. Check with your dealer when you have made the calculations.
✔ If the flow of water from a pump is too restricted it can heat up and damage the coils. Make sure that there is a bypass system fitted which allows the pressurized water to flow back into the pond. These are supplied with most pond pumps.

Non-submersible electric pumps

These are mainly used in industrial situations where large quantities of water are to be moved long distances. Easily maintained, they have the disadvantage of being noisy and require soundproofed housings which are liable to flood if placed below ground level.

Ram pumps

Where there is a natural flow of water near your pond, you may consider the use of ram pumps, which were widely used in the 19th and early 20th centuries. Using the force of a downward running stream, they force a small quantity of water up an incline. Still occasionally used today, they have the disadvantage of making a sharp tapping noise, and are best used where electricity or solar power are not available to run a modern pump.

Pipework

Where conduits are required for filters or a balancing chamber, good quality pre-formed pipework should be used – the pipework used for drainage in domestic situations is inexpensive and readily available. Use the largest practical bore for the pipework, as it is less likely to block up and create problems for maintenance. Always test the joints and couplings as, when the pond is filled, the joints will be under considerable strain, (more than in a drainage situation), caused by the head of water attempting to expand and burst the joints.

For land drainage or allowing water to drain away, use flexible plastic pipes perforated with many small holes. These pipes should ideally be buried in gravel, which will allow water to percolate through and run off (see page 26).

Lighting

A large number of lights are available for both exterior and underwater use. These are generally low voltage and have a transformer. All cables should be carefully hidden and protected from damage by gardening implements such as pronged forks. Underwater lamps should be placed so that the lenses do not become covered with detritus in the water, or if that is not possible, position them so that they can easily be cleaned. Water diffuses light, so place lenses close to the surface of the water.

Controls

Lighting and pumps can be controlled remotely from the pond, ideally from a situation where you can see the pond. However it is important to protect the controls from the weather. In planning electrical controls, it is wise to consult an electrician at an early stage. Modern contact breakers and RCD units should be fitted to any external electrical units, and any power supplies should be conducted in armoured cables capable of handling the required amperage without difficulty. All external fittings should be of a waterproof or weatherproof approved standard.

Water supply

This is usually taken from the mains supply or a natural source such as a spring or stream. When an automatic topping-up system such as a ballcock is to be used, fit a non-return valve into the system in order to make it completely impossible for water to flow back from the pond into the mains supply (see page 27).

Pumps, pipes and lights

There is a large range of pumps available; generally the more you pay the better the quality. Your retailer will advise and ask two key questions: what amount of water is required and what height is it to be raised. Measure the height from the water surface to the outlet and explain the type of display you wish to achieve. Some outdoor light fittings can be used either around the edge of the pond, or as underwater lights.

Fountainhead
Some are adjustable like the nozzle on a garden hosepipe

Telescopic outlet pipe
Extends telescopically to suit different depths

Pipe reducer
For fitting different size fountain heads

Push-fit connector
Check that this is suitable for your set-up

Screw-fit connector
Ensures secure joints

T-junction
Facility for a tap and a second outlet pipe

Integral adjuster
Rotates to restrict flow

Reinforced garden hosepipe

Flexible armoured pipe

Flexible clear plastic pipe

Domestic drainage pipe

Perforated land drainage pipe

Joint for domestic drainage pipe (various angles available)

Order a spare bulb when you buy any lamps

Take care not to damage the liner when fixing the light

Cable outlet

Underwater light

The glass features a structured surface which breaks the light

Power selector

A bracket allows the light to be turned up to 180°

A garden spike can easily be attached to the bracket

Pump and filter housing

Submersible pump

Fixing plate

Exterior light

Construction materials

In general, the fewer the number and type of materials involved in the construction of a pond and surrounding area, the more pleasing it is to the eye. If any particular type of brick or stone is used near the pond, make sure that you will be able to obtain replacements at a later date, in case any of them are damaged. Where possible use local materials. Architectural salvage yards are always worth investigating.

Concrete and mortar

Concrete

Used to form solid foundations and footings, the strength of concrete is dictated by the ratio (by volume) of sand and stones (ballast) to cement powder. For most pond construction work a ratio of 4 parts ballast to 1 part cement is ideal, but if large areas are to be concreted, it is worth considering reinforcing the concrete with steel mesh. Most cement manufacturers will be happy to advise you.

The amount of water used in a concrete mix affects its handling properties: the more water used, the sloppier the concrete. Too much water will affect the strength of the cured concrete. For most practical pond work the concrete should stand rather like stiff mashed potatoes, and it should be used quickly after it has been mixed, before it stiffens up. There is a range of proprietary additives that affect its properties, but these are expensive and can affect the strength, and I would suggest avoiding them unless unusual circumstances prevail.

Concrete should not be mixed or used when frost or below-freezing temperatures are expected, as they make concrete crumble and become useless. If there is a possibility of frost once you've laid the concrete, protect it with sacking or insulating material which stop it from freezing. Equally, if high temperatures are anticipated, protect concrete from drying out too quickly, using plastic sheeting, damp hessian cloths or sacking.

Mortar

This is the sand-and-cement mixture that is used to bond bricks and blocks together. It can be made in a variety of types and strengths: for building brick walls a mixture of 3 parts builders' sand to 1 part cement is standard. This can be coloured if required, using readily available colorants.

Caution

The cement powder used to make concrete and mortar is corrosive. Always wear a dust-mask, gloves and goggles. If you get cement on your skin wash it off immediately with plenty of water.

Other materials

Gravel

Gravel is used for under-liner drainage as it allows water to pass through, and can also be used for beaches, paths and level areas. It is available in many grades, from fine pea gravel to gravel the size of a small egg. It can be bought washed or unwashed – the latter is cheaper.

Soil

Clay loam for putting in ponds should ideally be sterilized to kill any weed seeds that may be in it. Aquatic nurseries can supply small amounts; use sterilized, screened topsoil for large amounts.

Wood

Wood can be used for bridges, decking and garden buildings – and even as a surround for a formal pond. It is generally classified as either hardwood or softwood. Hardwood is slow-grown wood from deciduous trees such as oak, elm or ash, while softwoods are usually from pine or other evergreen trees. Most softwoods should be treated in order to stop them from rotting – especially if they are to be in contact with water. Check with the manufacturer that the treatment will not affect the fish or wildlife and avoid anything that has loose knots or splits.

Each type of tree has its own characteristics for strength, ease of handling and cutting, and resistance to water. Freshly cut oak (known as green oak), for instance, is ideal for decking applications as it lasts in water for more than 25 years. It takes on a lovely silver-grey colour, and is relatively inexpensive and easy to work. Avoid beech wood and most other hardwoods unless you have checked its resistance to rotting in water. Carpenters or your wood supplier will advise you.

Use stainless steel, brass or galvanised bolts and screws as others will corrode and damage the wood.

Walling materials

Generally walling which will be seen ("facing work") is more expensive than hidden materials. Often walls have a backing of inexpensive bricks or blocks with a facing of high-quality bricks or stonework. Natural materials should be used wherever possible. Stone generally ages better than pre-moulded materials although these are often less expensive and easier to work with. If you are in doubt, a builder's merchant will advise you.

Concrete blocks are generally weatherproof; however, some bricks are not resistant to water and frost and will fail if used in pond or exterior construction.

Calculating quantities

✔ Allow 10% over the calculated quantities to allow for wastage.

✔ Talk to your merchant before quantifying: some materials are measured in face square metres, some by weight and some by number of units.

✔ Concrete and mortar quantities quoted in this book refer to volumes (parts) and weights, eg. 1 part cement (25 kg) and 4 parts sand (100 kg). The weights are only a rough guide to ordering; always mix by volume.

Paving materials

A vast range is available at widely differing prices, with natural stone the most expensive. If purchasing natural stone to edge a pond, remember that, unlike in most other situations, the depth of the stone is important because the edges of the pavers will be seen, so consistency in depth should be specified.

Manufactured pavers, made to look like natural stone, are also available. The better ones age well and become indistinguishable from natural stone when lichens and other materials age them. Others lose their colour quickly and can become an eyesore, so choose carefully.

Construction materials

General DIY stores, builders' merchants and architectural salvage yards will have a wide range of bricks, stone, wood and fixings. Explain the purpose and use as some may be adversely affected by water. You will find variations in price so check with different manufacturers. Sometimes you can reduce costs by changing the design.

Brick

Boulder

Slate

Natural stone paving

Gravel

Coach bolt, washer and nut

Galvanised steel nail

Cobbles

Coated screw

Manufactured paving

Softwood post, plank and other useful sections

Sleeper

Tools

Tools are one of the main keys to successful pond-building. Although the best tools are no substitute for enthusiasm and determination, carefully chosen, top-quality tools will ensure that each and every task is accomplished with minimum effort and maximum efficiency, in the shortest possible time. It is fine to begin by using your existing tools for the projects – buy new ones if and when the need arises.

Level

Because water levels are flat it is vital that the edge of a pond is also built flat. The easiest way to achieve this is to use a long spirit level (1–2 m long is suitable) which can also be used in conjunction with a straight beam of wood. For large ponds (5 m in diameter or more) a number of wooden pegs can be hit in the ground and levelled with each other. A surveyor's level will give improved accuracy.

Excavator

Depending on the scale of your project and the availability of access, you can rent a tracked excavating machine, with or without an operator. The size and type of mechanical digger required for a job is related to the amount of work to be done – generally a 360-degree tracked excavator, ranging in size from 1 to 32 tons, is suitable. Your hire shop will be able to make recommendations when you outline the size of the excavations and your needs for handling material. If you are hiring a dumper truck, make sure it is not too small for the job; again, advice from the hire company will be helpful.

Try to plan the work so that you do not disturb more ground than is necessary, starting in one area and working your way out. Precision with levels is important, as replaced subsoil is not as structurally sound as the virgin ground. Keep others well outside the danger areas where you are working.

Where the ground is soft and the area less than 3 m in diameter, digging by hand is the best way to create a pond. For larger areas consider using an excavator.

Hand digging tools

Chose your tools with care – a well-chosen, quality tool is a worthwhile investment. A good spade is particularly important if you are excavating the pond manually. For very hard ground you will need a spade with a narrow cutting edge but if the soil is friable you may approach with a shovel. Most hardware stores carry a good range. Generally metal tools are less expensive and more durable than wood or plastic handled tools. Gently does it if you are not in the habit of digging. You will use muscles unused to work so half an hour is the maximum you should work on the first outing; build up carefully after that. A sturdy wheelbarrow is an essential tool that will make lifting and carrying easier. Make sure you get the right size of wheelbarrow for the job: one that can be handled easily when full but is still large enough to be useful.

Concrete mixers

Although small quantities of concrete can be mixed by hand, the work is much eased by using a powered concrete mixer. These are generally powered by electricity or a petrol engine. If electricity is available close to the workings, an electric mixer should be your preferred option as they are quieter and cheaper to run. Make sure you have a circuit breaker plugged into the power socket to protect you from electric shock if an accident occurs.

It is important to wash out the mixer thoroughly after each load is used up as otherwise the mortar or concrete will set in the drum and reduce efficiency as well as incur a cleaning cost when the machine is returned to the hirer.

Safety equipment

- ✔ Sturdy boots with steel toecaps, available at builder's merchants, are necessary for all pond construction.

- ✔ Gloves are vital during work with concrete, as your skin may react if in contact with concrete or mortar.

- ✔ Goggles are required if you are operating any grinding equipment, as is ear protection if you have to hire noisy machines.

- ✔ If you are involving an excavator, wear a hard hat:

- ✔ Make sure you have the number of the local hospital handy, and keep a first-aid kit close to hand.

A basic tool kit

A good set of tools makes pond building easy and the right tool can save you a lot of time. For the projects in this book, you will need a bucket, a wheelbarrow and some of the tools shown below. All of these can be bought from a local general DIY superstore, or hired. Some specialist tools, such as a pick or mattock for hard ground are not shown but hire shop staff can advise on what you might need. A wooden board of about 500 mm square will be helpful for placing mortar on for brick laying. Rubble bags and a broom will be necessary for tiding up.

Gloves

Large tape measure

Pegs and string

Scissors

Line set

Mortar trowel

Bolster chisel

Pointing trowel

Grinder

Brick hammer

Club hammer

Spirit level

Spade

Fork

Shovel

Sledgehammer

Rake

Square

Tape measure

Carpenter's pencil

General saw

Drill

Drill bit

Claw hammer

Adjustable spanner

Cordless driver

Caution
Power tools
Electricity, early-morning dew, buckets of water and wet hands are a potentially dangerous combination. When you use a power tool or an electric cement mixer, make sure that you use it in conjunction with an electricity circuit breaker and switch off the power when not in use.

Basic techniques

Pond building can be good fun especially when you have a clear understanding of the basic techniques such as marking out, laying concrete and building brick walls, and when you can handle the tools and materials with confidence. If you have never made garden projects before, start with something small and simple. If you need encouragement why not plan a big pond and get some friends to help?

Dress right for the job

Old clothes are fine, as they will get dirty, however overalls are readily available and have many useful pockets. A sound pair of boots is essential, personally I favour boots which have a steel toecap and are easy to get on and off. Gloves should be worn if your hands are soft or you are dealing with materials like concrete, which can irritate the skin.

Take plenty of breaks

Stop for at least ten minutes every hour to assess your progress, have a pause and plan the next stage. Do your calculations and order materials when you are fresh and take photographs of each stage of the progress; you will be able to show them

Getting started

proudly in years to come. Take your time, and bring in help if some part of the job will over stretch you. If you come across obstacles like huge rocks consider keeping them as part of your design.

Measuring and marking

Use the carpenter's maxim "measure it twice and cut it once" and always make a note of your measurements.

Keep a good-quality carpenter's pencil handy for marking out on wood.

When ordering bricks, blocks, sand and concrete allow 10% for wastage.

Road marking paints of various colours are available from builders' merchants and are ideal for marking out lines. Clear the nozzles after each use.

A taut string line will ensure accurate digging

Before proceeding be absolutely confident in your setting out. Do not hurry this stage as any mistake will be difficult and costly to rectify and require fruitless labour.

Foundations

The purpose of foundations is to provide a level and stable base on which to build. Foundations should generally be twice as wide as the wall that is to be built on them. The depth of the foundations varies but for most pond work 250 mm is deep enough; however if the base material is unstable, or liable to crack and heave such as clay, it is wise to err on the side of caution and dig down to 500 mm. Fill the majority of the void with hardcore and compact it by beating it down with a heavy hammer or by using a vibrating compaction machine before filling up to the required depth with concrete.

Foundations need to be level; pegs set at the same level can be used as a guide to spreading the concrete

This trench will be filled with a layer of hardcore and topped off with concrete

Most ponds require foundations and these are either "footings" (a narrow strip of concrete) or a slab. If you don't build foundations the pond may quickly disintegrate.

Laying concrete

Always wear gloves as splashes can irritate and burn the skin. If you do get concrete on your skin wash it off with plenty of water immediately.

When you are moving the concrete from the mixer to the point of laying, do not overfill the barrow, as any slops will be unsightly, kill grass and be difficult to clean up afterwards. Also a heavy wheelbarrow full of liquid can be hard to control over uneven ground.

Start in one corner and work backwards, achieving the finished level with your float or tamping bar before moving on to the next section. In the same way as you would ice a cake, put an appropriate amount of concrete in the middle and then spread and manipulate the concrete making sure that you have sufficient before pushing it down to the final level. Work only in one direction at a time and do not leave any unfinished sections before moving on. Do not be rushed by the person delivering the concrete to you (if you are so lucky) and leave it in the barrow until you are ready to receive it.

When you have finished laying a section, immediately clean all your tools and put the unused concrete to good use. Never be tempted to bury it.

Use a piece of wood to "tamp" the concrete level

Make sure that you have prepared the area before you start pouring concrete. Building a level wooden frame called "formwork" is sometimes the easiest option.

Brick work

The main thing is to build the wall upright, in the right place and with all the layers or courses of brick or block horizontal with staggered vertical joints.

The key to success is in the mixing of the mortar, which ideally should have the consistency of stiff mashed potatoes; if it is too dry the bricks will not readily bond to it. However, if it is too wet, the bricks will slide about. If possible watch a bricklayer at work and try to emulate his mortar. Be careful not to add too much water at the end of the mixing process as if the mix becomes too wet the only way to stiffen it up is to add more sand and cement, which can easily result in the over filling of the mixer.

Trial and error is the only way to learn, however once you have got it right once it is easy to do the same thing again, a bit like riding a bicycle.

Use a string line to show where the bricks should be laid by wrapping the string around a brick, pulling the line over another and pulling the ends apart until the line is straight. Do a dry run without any mortar just touching (or kissing) the line with the bricks without moving the line.

Allow for a 15 mm bed of mortar below the bottom brick and carefully re-set the line so that the top edge of the brick will kiss the line.

Remove the bricks and lay down the mortar so that the entire bottom of the brick is on mortar. Place each brick frog uppermost on to the mortar and bed it down until it is in the correct position. Place some mortar on the ends of each brick before placing it so that you will have a 10 mm joint between each brick. If a brick is too low, lift it from the mortar bed, add fresh mortar and re-bed it.

Do not hurry the early process, it will rapidly become easier. Once laid a brick should not be touched again as that movement will break the seal between the brick and the mortar; if this happens the brick must be removed and the mortar and the brick replaced. So be careful not to knock any new brickwork. Do not begin laying the next brick until you are completely satisfied that the last one is correctly positioned.

When a row of bricks is complete, remove the excess mortar by slicing it off with the trowel.

The pattern of the brickwork is called the bond and it is this decorative arrangement of bricks that gives a wall its strength; it is important that the vertical joints do not occur near each other, as it weakens the wall and looks unsightly.

Tap each brick down until it is straight and level

Bricks and mortar are the ingredients for a classic raised pond. Position the bricks carfully, avoid smearing them with mortar, and do a nice job of finishing the joints.

Preparing the pond area for lining

Because butyl and other liners are damaged by sharp objects such as flints it is critical that during the building of a pond they are protected. Old carpet (of a synthetic, non-rotting type) can be used as an underlay, although modern geotextiles are readily available and easier to work with in a secure way (see page 17).

Consider the subsoil where the pond is to be. If it is naturally draining and is not affected by the local water table, no further action need be taken; however, if the subsoil may hold some water (such as clay or shale for example) or the natural water table may come up during the winter, you will need to create an escape for any water that might accumulate under the liner. Dig a trench 300 mm wide by 300 mm deep from the lowest point in the excavation, following the contours of the excavation towards the (downhill) lowest side of the site. End the trench 800 mm outside the excavated area. Place a 100 mm perforated land drain in the trench and fill with 10 mm gravel.

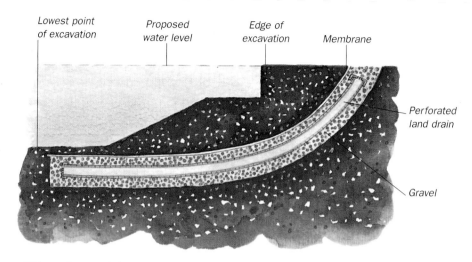

Lowest point of excavation *Proposed water level* *Edge of excavation* *Membrane* *Perforated land drain* *Gravel*

If the soil around the pond holds some water or if the natural water table rises in winter, a water escape trench will help deal with the water accumulating under the liner.

Pond lining

Positioning a flexible liner

With the liner roughly in place, take an edge in both hands and raise and lower it sharply. This produces a cushion of air between the liner and the geotextile and allows the liner to be drawn towards you. Repeat until the liner is correctly positioned, checking that the geotextile has not been dislodged during the process. Stop further wind affecting the liner by weighing it down at the sides, taking care not to allow any sharp objects to come into contact with the liner. Fill the pond with enough water to hold the bottom securely, and tug at the edges to minimize any creases and folds (see page 17).

Fitting a non-flexible liner

The important thing is not to leave any voids beneath the liner, as when it is filled with water it will be strained and may crack. Try to dig the hole to match the shape of the shell, allowing for at least 25 mm of sand all round. When you have achieved this, shovel a small amount of sand all around the excavation. By placing and removing the shell you will be able to see all the places where the sand has touched the shell allowing you to build up the sand in areas where it has not touched. By repeating this procedure of adding and removing sand, the bottom section of the shell should sit evenly on a bed of sand. When you are satisfied that no more can be done by this method finally place the shell and fill up the voids at the side using a stick to push the sand and compact it. When the edges are nearly full put a hosepipe into the sand and when the area is soaking compact the sand where you can to fill any remaining voids. It is then safe to fill the pond.

A line of bricks can be used to form a retaining edge to a planting shelf

Protective geotextile is used under the bricks and under the butyl

Fill the pond with enough water to weigh down the butyl

A flexible liner such as butyl is suitable for any pond shape and should be laid on top of soft geotextile. Additional geotextile is used wherever there is risk of damaging the butyl.

Repairing leaks in a flexible liner

Butyl liners can leak either because something is penetrating the liner or because it is undergoing stress brought about by stretching. In either case ensure that the cause is dealt with before undertaking the repair. The main difficulty lies in exposing the hole and making sure the surrounding area is clean and dry before you begin repairing the hole. A patch is made by attaching joining tape to a pre-sized piece of butyl, leaving the waxed paper on the tape until the last possible moment. Although this is a fairly straightforward job it can be challenging on a muddy wet construction site, especially as cleanliness is essential to make permanent waterproof joints. Offer up the liners for joining making sure that the join will not be under strain when complete. Wash away any earth or materials that have stuck to the liner and clean an area at least 100 mm around where the join is to be made. Use petrol to further clean the surfaces to be joined. Make sure the surfaces are dry with no rucks or pleats before taping together. Place the double-sided rubber tape between the cleaned surfaces. Using a blowlamp, warm the joined area by constantly moving the heat source so as not to burn the surface. When an area of about 300 mm is warmed up turn off the blowlamp and wearing light gloves knead the join to ensure complete adhesion to both surfaces. Repeat the process on the next section of the join until the join is complete. Using scissors trim off any material left over next to the completed join. Carry out any repairs on a hot dry day.

Automatic top-up system

During dry summer months, the level of water in a pond may drop considerably. It can easily be topped up using a hose pipe, however, on butyl-lined ponds an automatic system can be built into the pond during construction. This uses the mains water supply to keep the water level in the pond continually at the optimum level. This is particularly useful when the pond has fountains, streams or waterfalls which increase water evaporation.

Once you have excavated your pond, but before it has been lined, you will need to select the position for the automatic top-up chamber. This should be on rising ground ideally not more than 2 m from the edge of the pond. Buy a multibase drains inspection unit and enough 100 mm rigid pipe to reach from the chamber into the pond. These are available from most builders' merchants.

Excavate a hole large enough to contain the chamber and set it so that the top rim is at least 100 mm above the proposed water level in the pond. Stop up any unused pipe penetrations into the chamber. I use clear silicon around the clean stopper as an additional measure.

Dig a trench which leads from the chamber to the pond and attach the rigid pipe to the chamber so that it leads into the pond. Backfill around the chamber and pipe using soft sand.

When you come to line the pond you will need to cut a hole in the liner to allow the pipe to penetrate through without allowing water out. You can do this by buying a purpose-made penetration sleeve from the supplier of the butyl. This can be attached to the liner using double-sided tape and heated to ensure a watertight joint. Bury flexible water pipe from the source of supply to the chamber. In colder climates this should be trenched in not less than 500 mm below ground to stop it from freezing during the winter. Connect the water supply to the mains. When the pond is filled the water level in the chamber will be at the same level as the pond. Affix to the side of the pond a domestic ballcock adjusted so that the supply is turned off when the pond is full but turned on when the water level falls.

Brick
A brick box to enable easy access

Ballcock
Switches the water supply on and off automatically; the hollow ball floats but is also being forced downwards by a spring so that it moves with the water level and switches the water on (when the ball is down) and off (when the ball is up)

Mains water supply
Water pipe is connected to the stopcock valve

Sand backfill

Rigid pipe
Leading to the bottom of the pond

Proposed water level

Inspection chamber
This and other components can be bought from a builder's merchant

An automatic top-up system like this one can be used for large ponds where there is a concern that the water level may drop rapidly in periods of hot dry weather.

Planting and development

The planting of a pond is, like the furnishing and decorating of a house, entirely a matter of personal taste. You may prefer an immediate complete scheme or to plant very simply and develop the project over a number of years, with each change or addition holding some personal significance or reflecting changing personal taste. The main thing is to find a knowledgeable plant supplier with a good range of stock.

Choosing plants

A mature pond with well established plants, rather in need of some routine maintenance and thinning. The ideal is to have one third of the surface of the water covered with plants as too much shaded area lowers the oxygen levels of the pond. Overcrowded plants are more prone to pests and diseases.

Plants can be moved easily, and the scheme can be altered as the various plants develop. Bold clumps with just a few classic plants generally have a more pleasing effect than a large number of different species. Simpler is generally better although your choice of plants will depend on the style of your pond.

Many aquatic plants are available by mail order. There are five categories:
- ✔ Submerged, also known as oxygenators or pondweeds
- ✔ Floating
- ✔ Floating-leaved
- ✔ Emergent or bog
- ✔ Waterside

Submerged plants (oxygenators or pondweeds)

These are the first plants that should be put into a newly completed pond for two reasons. First, they start putting oxygen into the water and grow rapidly during the growing season; and second, they generally have secondary forms of pond life in them, such as water fleas and daphnia which, as long as there is no competition, rapidly reproduce, creating a richer environment that encourages other forms of beneficial pond life.

It is worth visiting your local pond shop to see what oxygenators they have available, but take care that they are native to your environment, as some imported plants can grow rampantly and are unable to provide food or shelter for native forms of pond life.

Weigh down oxygenators with small metal collars (which can be obtained from aquatic supply shops) so that they take root at the bottom of the pond. Excessive amounts of pondweed should be thinned out during the summer months, by hand or using a plastic rake.

Floating plants

These obtain their nutrients from fine root hairs that they suspend in the water. It is important that floating plants are not allowed to cover too much of the surface of the pond, as they can stifle the submerged plants that depend on light filtering down through the water. If they become over-vigorous, they can be raked out. Some plants are liable to frost damage and should be brought indoors during periods of extreme cold.

Floating-leaved plants

One of the most popular floating-leaved plants are water lilies with round or oval leaves, which are suitable for any depth of water up to 1.75 m deep. There is a wide range available with a variety of leaf sizes, and if you live in a tropical region, a more exotic range is available.

Floating-leaved plants
The leaves and flowers float on the water surface

Submerged plants
Fronds put oxygen into the water

Baskets sitting on the bottom of the pond

Submerged plants and floating-leaved plants both need to be rooted at the bottom of the pond (refer to plant labels).

Emergent plants
On shelves at the side of the pond

Bog plants
Planted in water-soaked earth

Emergent and bog plants have very different needs – read the plant labels and ask for advice before purchasing them.

Waterside plants
These plants like continuously damp (but not wet) soil

Waterside plants require frequent watering until they are established. Choose larger species for a dramatic effect.

Floating-leaved plants should be grown in pots placed upright on the bottom of the pond at levels to suit. Remove excess and dying leaves, cutting the stems as low as practical in the water.

Lilies need to be thinned and divided after a number of years. Lift the plants in their baskets to the side of the pond and, using pruning shears, cut the corms into two sections, making sure that both halves have roots, flower heads and leaves. Cut back long or damaged roots and replant in clay or aquatic soil in perforated pots with the corm just showing above the soil, and cover with gravel to hold the earth in place.

Emergent and bog plants

Planted on planting shelves, bog areas or in containers at the edge of a pond, perennial emergent plants grow up quickly in the spring and die down in the autumn. Some forms of plants, such as rushes and grasses, which remain standing in the winter, will provide colour and form during the winter months. They should be divided in the autumn after two or three years. Some plants require different care and conditions so read the labels carefully and plant accordingly.

Waterside plants

These may be much larger than the emergent and bog plants that grow at the water's edge. During the winter months they offer contrasting scale, colour and form, and may produce reflections off the water. It must be remembered that, although they are next to the pond, they are outside the wet area and are unable to take water from the pond so that they may require additional watering during the early years while they establish themselves and develop. Be aware that while some plants might be described as waterside plants – like some species of bamboo – they are so fast growing that the sharp roots can damage a flexible pond lining. You should build a barrier or avoid them.

Maintenance

The hard slog of building the pond may be over, but regular, simple maintenance is vital if it is both to look its best and attract the wildlife that develop a working ecosystem (see page 32). But what could be better on a bright spring day than to put on rubber boots and splodge around in water and mud? Take this opportunity to inspect pumps and pipework, clean out clogged filters and make necessary repairs.

Pond maintenance

Every pond will need some kind of maintenance, although deep ponds tend to remain cleaner than shallow ones. Most of the jobs are quick and easy to do and are aimed at removing obvious debris like leaves and twigs, checking the balance of plant life which may entail raking away algae, weeding out over-dominant plants and reducing the number of fish. Occasionally you will need to change the water and repair any damaged liner (see page 27).

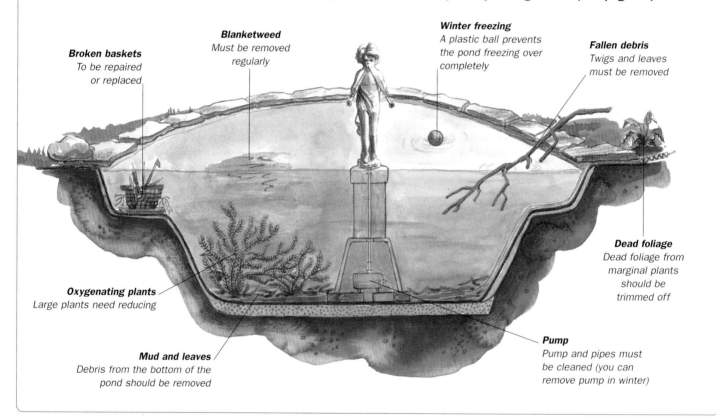

Broken baskets
To be repaired
or replaced

Blanketweed
Must be removed
regularly

Winter freezing
A plastic ball prevents
the pond freezing over
completely

Fallen debris
Twigs and leaves
must be removed

Dead foliage
Dead foliage from
marginal plants
should be
trimmed off

Oxygenating plants
Large plants need reducing

Mud and leaves
Debris from the bottom of the
pond should be removed

Pump
Pump and pipes must
be cleaned (you can
remove pump in winter)

Routine maintenance

Controlling algae

Algae, particularly blanketweed, often proliferates on a garden pond, particularly when it is new and has not achieved a balanced ecosystem or is overstocked with fish. While there are a large number of preparations and suggestions for controlling algae, many of these have detrimental long-term effects. During the spring and early summer, remove algae on a frequent basis, using a plastic garden rake. As the growing season progresses and the pond's ecosystem develops, algae will grow with less vigour.

Plant maintenance

Controlling plants, so that one species does not dominate and inhibit other plants, can be done throughout the growing season as need dictates. In particular, floating-leaved plants should be watched carefully. Weeding unwanted species should be done little and often on a weekly basis, especially during the spring.

Fallen leaves floating on the pond surface sink in time and add to the detritus that accumulates at the bottom of a pond. In order to delay the time when a pond needs clearing out, these should be raked off and removed. For a small pond a net, spread over the pond's surface during the autumn, will facilitate this task.

Cut back and remove dead plant life during the autumn or, if you prefer, late in winter, just before the spring growing season. If the pond has a liner avoid using sharp-pronged metal tools and generally take care not to cause damage.

When to clean out

Because of the constant input of detritus into ponds, all need cleaning out from time to time, otherwise you will notice after some years that the characteristics of the pond become altered – the water becomes dark and cloudy, and the plants and wildlife that used to thrive start to die out. Cleaning work is generally best done in the spring or early summer, not least because the water is warmer and more pleasant to deal with.

Clearing and cleaning the pond

Start by pumping out the pond, using a submersible pump with a flexible hose, taking care to run the water into a drain or somewhere it can percolate away slowly without doing damage. Take care to preserve the fish or wildlife that you find as the water level drops, transferring the

Occasional maintenance

fish to a temporary container (a clean plastic dustbin is suitable), making sure that the water in it is well provided with oxygen, or the fish may suffocate. Putting an air pump into the holding container generally takes care of this problem.

Once the pump has taken out all the water that it can without becoming blocked, remove the rest of the detritus using a bucket and soft scoop. There is a real danger of damaging pond liners whilst they are unprotected by water, so make sure that no metal or sharp objects are used in this operation; also make sure that no sharp stones are trapped in the soles of boots. Do not be tempted to use any detergents or cleansing agents.

Remove the majority of the detritus – but not all. It is important to allow a certain amount to remain, as it contains enough of the microscopic pond life to

Care of fish

Remove and re-site fish if they have bred and their numbers and size are greater than originally planned. They are easiest to catch in the autumn, as the water temperature lowers and they become sluggish. If a pond is overstocked, fish become prey to disease and stresses. It is no kindness to the fish to allow them to breed and grow without control.

Fountainhead
Clear any blockages with a pin

Foam filter
Switch off the power, take the casing apart and rinse out thoroughly with clean water

Clean your pump regularly. If dirt and weed build up in the filter, the pump will fail.

recolonize the pond. Cleared detritus should be allowed to dry beside the pond and then be removed in sacks or placed on a compost heap, where it will rot down to provide an excellent compost.

Now is an excellent time to carefully assess the plants and divide any whose root systems are now accessible.

Any pumps and pipes should be carefully inspected and cleaned or replaced.

Restocking the pond

The pond can be refilled with water from a hosepipe or, in ideal circumstances, with stored rainwater. Consider the number of fish that you have taken out of the pond and re-site some if necessary. Allow as long as possible before reintroducing fish into the pond to allow the water temperature to stabilize and give the ecosystem a chance to re-establish.

When you buy new plants use a quarantine bucket which allows you to select precisely what you do and don't want in your pond.

Blanketweed
Blanketweed must be removed

Decaying plants
All dead plant material pulled away

Water boatman
Small predator fish taken out

Plants
Washed before being put into the pond

Freshwater shrimp
A perfect resident for a pond

Balancing the ecosystem

Natural life will come quickly to your pond, and the ecosystem within it will start to develop as soon as it is filled. It is important not to disrupt this development by prematurely introducing fish or birds that short-circuit the ongoing development of the life of the pond. For a natural-looking pond you should choose plants and fish that are native to your area and avoid adding too many plants in the first instance.

Developing an ecosystem

The speed and development of the pond life are affected by three major factors relating to the water: nutrients, temperature and oxygen. These can be gradually manipulated through design, planting, stocking and maintenance to achieve the desired effect.

Nutrients in the water

These arrive in water, from the air, from rotting and dying plant material and from the excretions of fish and birds. If there are too many nutrients, the natural cycles which cope with the detritus break

This pond requires some basic maintenance (see page 30). The plants could be reduced, there is a lot of detritus that needs removing and surface weed that can be removed.

down, the water becomes entirely opaque and the system starts to smell unpleasant. In addition, nutrients in the water and high water temperature encourage the growth of algae, especially in the spring before pond plants have developed to absorb the excess nutrients.

Problems with algae are best avoided rather than cured. This can be done in a number of ways:

- Design the pond so that water that may have fertiliser dissolved in it does not run into it.
- Make the pond deep and large enough so that the water temperature does not rise too high.
- Plant shade-providing and nutrient-absorbing plants in and around the pond.
- Do not overstock with fish or birds.
- Provide consistent maintenance (see page 30).
- Inject oxygen into the water to aid the breaking down of nutrients.

Water temperature

This is to a great extent dictated by the weather and ambient temperature; however, the deeper the pond, the less immediately responsive it will be to day-to-day changes in the weather, and the more stable it will become. There is a natural cycle, rather like the weather, in which water circulates, bringing oxygen in the water to all parts, encouraging plants and wildlife, and helping with the breaking down of nutrients. It is principally for this reason that it is worth digging a pond as deep as is practical. Although you may be tempted to reduce costs by saving in depth, in the long term this always leads to a reduction in stability and to increased maintenance costs. Something of the same effect of depth of water can be achieved by pumping oxygen into the water; however, as with all artificial environments, it can never be as desirable or stable as an environment that works simply with nature.

Oxygen in the water

As for us, oxygen provides life in a pond: it is absorbed by the water from air passing over it, water spilling through air, and by the photosynthesis of plants in the water. The more oxygen there is in pond water, the healthier it will be and the more life it will sustain. It also aids the decomposition of detritus in the pond, helping to keep the environment healthy and dynamic.

Oxygen can be injected into water to aid the breaking down of nutrients. This can be done either by using an air pump to pump air to the bottom of the pond, as we see with domestic fish tanks, or by throwing the water into the air, as with fountains and waterfalls.

Water filtration for fish

If a pond is designed for wildlife it will be able to sustain a small number of ornamental fish without upsetting the ecology and appearance of the pond. If however, fish are to be the predominant life in the pond, and there is no freshwater supply, you will need to install a filtration system. Filtration systems, often housed in a specially constructed unit adjacent to the pond – remove nutrients in suspension or solution in the water by passing the water over a series of filters before being returned to the pond. They are usually made up from a sponge or filter to remove sizeable solids from the water and a biological filter which works in the same way as a sewage plant by passing the water over a large surface area containing bacteria which absorb and convert nutrients into a non toxic form. In addition, an ultraviolet light kills bacteria growing in the water.

In addition to filtration, air may be pumped into the water to add to its oxygen content. If you fancy adding a dramatic feature to the pond then a waterfall, cascade or fountain also keeps the water oxygenated and fresh.

A beautiful example of a natural-looking pond. Clear water, thriving plants (maybe some of the plants could be reduced), the presence of fish, frogs, gnats, water snails and dragonflies, all suggest that the ecosystem of the pond is well balanced.

Part 2
Projects

Natural Pond

Perhaps the simplest and least expensive type of pond to create, a natural pond will fit in almost anywhere where there is a lawn or flat area in the garden. Carefully sited, it can offer stunning reflections, bringing the sky down to the earth as well as the delights of plant life both on and below the surface of the water. Once planted, wildlife will quickly come, be it frogs, newts, dragonflies or water beetles.

★
Easy

Making time
3 weekends
Three days for digging the hole and three days for lining and building the edges

Considering the design

If you have decided that this is the pond for you, consider the impact it will have on your garden. Ideally you need a completely flat, level surface but it can be positioned where there is a slight slope, as we did. As long as your foundation trench is level, it doesn't matter if part of your pond edge wall is above ground level; simply fill the area behind the wall. A good idea is to mark out the area of pond (as large as possible) and imagine what you would do in your garden with the pond in place. Only once you are convinced of the practicality and correct siting of the pond should you proceed. Consider what you are going to do with the spoil, how you are going to move it and by what route and tell the neighbours of your plans.

Getting started

Assemble your materials and equipment. Choose a dry day but make sure that you have somewhere to store your cement (off the ground and covered with waterproof material) should it suddenly rain while the work is in progress. Remember the final shape and depth of your pond will alter any quantities given.

You will need

Materials

- ✔ Concrete: 1 part cement (150 kg) and 4 parts ballast (600 kg)
- ✔ Sand: 1000 kg
- ✔ Geotextile: 46 sq metres
- ✔ Butyl: 1 piece 6 m x 6 m
- ✔ Bricks: 200
- ✔ Mortar: 1 part cement (25 kg) and 3 parts sand (75 kg)

Tools

- ✔ Tape measure, spray marker and pegs
- ✔ Wheelbarrow and bucket
- ✔ Spade, fork and shovel
- ✔ Club hammer
- ✔ Spirit level
- ✔ Pickaxe or mattock
- ✔ Rake
- ✔ Scissors
- ✔ Bricklayer's trowel

Overall dimensions and general notes

The design results in a completely natural-looking pond with no lining visible at the sides

The pond is approximately 4 m long and 3.3 m wide

Up to a third of the water's surface may be covered with plants once the pond has matured. Keep at least one aspect of the pond free for marginal planting.

Cross-section detail of the natural pond

Outer edge
See drawing below

Planting shelf

1:3 slope
Slopes downwards
300 mm every 900 mm

Depth
Dig the pond out to a
depth of about 800 mm

300 mm

300 mm

Cut-away detail of the natural pond

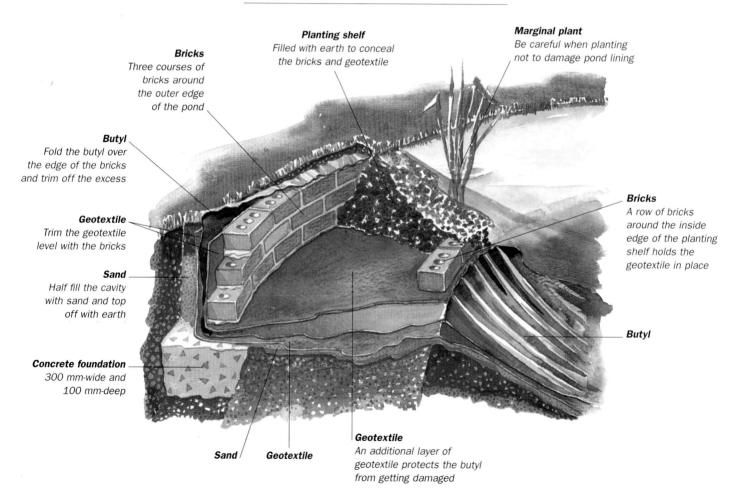

Bricks
Three courses of
bricks around
the outer edge
of the pond

Planting shelf
Filled with earth to conceal
the bricks and geotextile

Marginal plant
Be careful when planting
not to damage pond lining

Butyl
Fold the butyl over
the edge of the bricks
and trim off the excess

Bricks
A row of bricks
around the inside
edge of the planting
shelf holds the
geotextile in place

Geotextile
Trim the geotextile
level with the bricks

Sand
Half fill the cavity
with sand and top
off with earth

Butyl

Concrete foundation
300 mm-wide and
100 mm-deep

Sand **Geotextile**

Geotextile
An additional layer of
geotextile protects the butyl
from getting damaged

Cut-away plan view of the natural pond

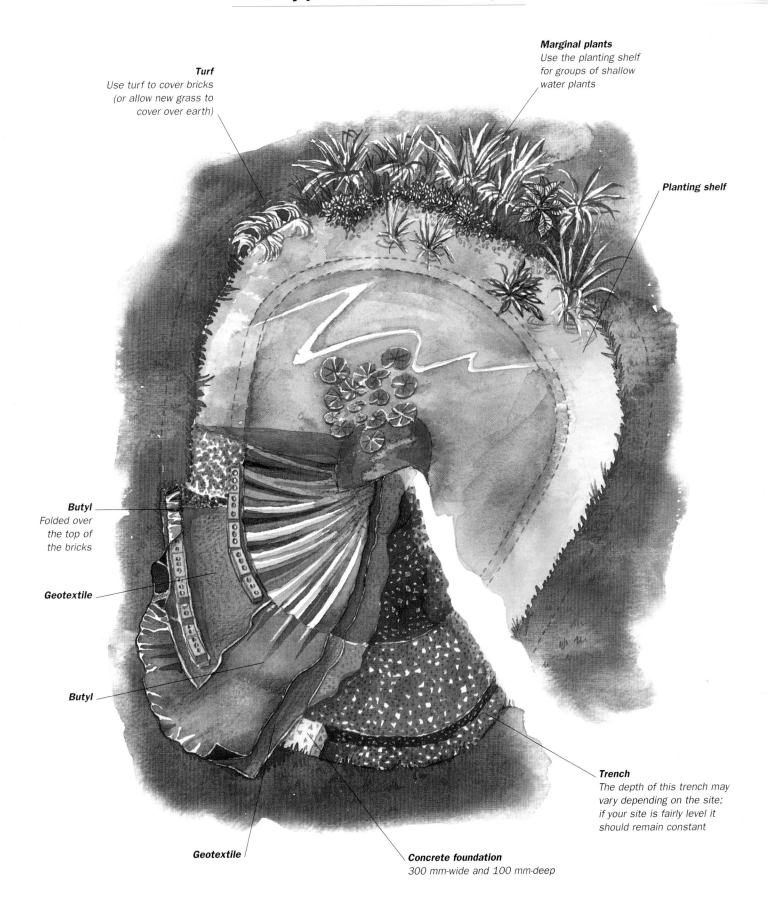

Turf
Use turf to cover bricks (or allow new grass to cover over earth)

Marginal plants
Use the planting shelf for groups of shallow water plants

Planting shelf

Butyl
Folded over the top of the bricks

Geotextile

Butyl

Geotextile

Concrete foundation
300 mm-wide and 100 mm-deep

Trench
The depth of this trench may vary depending on the site; if your site is fairly level it should remain constant

Making the natural pond

1 **Digging the foundation trench**
Use the tape measure and spray marker to set the shape of the pond out on a level area of ground. Use the spade to dig a narrow trench to a level depth of about 300 mm all around the pond. If your site does slope ensure the trench is a minimum of 300 mm deep.

2 **Setting out a level footing**
Check that the bottom of your trench is roughly level all around. Hammer in a series of wooden pegs approximately 800 mm apart so that they poke above the ground by 100 mm and the tops of the pegs are all exactly level with each other.

3 **Filling the trench**
Fill the trench with concrete up as far as the level of the top of the wooden pegs. The level brick wall will go on top of this concrete so make sure that you have spread the concrete evenly. A slightly sloping site may require building up with earth after the wall is built.

4 **Excavating the pond**
Using the pickaxe or mattock, spade and shovel, dig the pond out to a maximum depth of about 800 mm – complete with a planting shelf and a 1:3 slope (refer to the drawings on page 38).

5 **Laying the geotextile**
Remove all loose earth and sharp stones and cover the entire surface with a bed of raked sand. Cover the sand and the foundation with geotextile.

6 Laying the butyl
Carefully spread the butyl liner over the whole pond (see page 26 for useful tips), ensuring you have at least 300 mm of liner overlapping the edge of the pond all around. Pour a small quantity of water into the pond to hold the liner in place.

7 Edging the planting shelf
Cover the planting shelf with scraps of geotextile. Lay a row of bricks (without mortar) around the inner edge of the planting shelf to hold the geotextile in place. Do not worry about these bricks being visible – they will soon get covered in mud.

8 Building the pond edge wall
Lay three courses of mortared bricks around the outer edge of the pond, checking the level with each course. Add a mixture of mud and waste mortar in blobs around the inner edge of the dry bricks.

9 Trimming the lining
Fold the geotextile and butyl sandwich up and over the outer wall towards the middle of the pond. Fill the cavity between the wall and the surrounding earth with sand (do not use sharp tools). Trim the geotextile layers level with the top of the wall.

10 Finishing
Fill the planting shelf with earth, dig in your plants and top up with water. If the wall stands above the level of the ground, build up the area behind it with soil. Leave the butyl overlapping the wall and cover the exposed edge of the pond with spare topsoil or new turf.

Planted stream

Where there is sloping ground, a natural-looking planted stream is an option. This can lead down to a pond (one like the natural pond on page 36 is suitable) from which water can be pumped. It can meander with pools and eddies if the slope is a gentle one, or have waterfalls if the ground is steeper. The sound of the water can add to the delight of an environment that a wide range of interesting plants will thrive in.

★
Easy

Making time
3 weekends
4 days for digging and lining and a weekend to complete

Considering the design

The slope will affect the nature of your stream and the lie of the land; remember that water cannot run uphill! Study natural streams to see how a stream runs between obstacles and runs faster where the ground is steeper. If there are any natural clefts or gullies in your garden make use of them or move them to where you want your stream to be. Make sure the stream sits in, rather than on the surrounding landscape. Most problems arise when the stream is running and the water rises above the butyl at the edges! You will need constant power and water supplies for this project. Remember that a toddler can drown in as little as 10 mm of water so even a shallow stream like this one can pose a potential danger. Never leave children unsupervised.

Getting started

Plan the route of your stream and establish that the starting point is higher than the finishing point, that the sides of the liner will be at least 100 mm higher than the finished water level (even when the stream is running) and that this is below the ground level around the stream. Where rocks are to be placed to form a pool and waterfall the water will rise up to 50 mm above the obstruction.

Overall dimensions and general notes

Stones constrict the flow of the water and make more splash

Fish are drawn towards the bubbling oxygen-rich water as it enters the pond

Run the stream into an existing pond or build a new one (see the natural pond on page 36) about 2 m in diameter or larger. The materials listed will make a stream about 10 m long and 600 mm wide.

You will need

Materials

- ✔ Flexible armoured pipe: 50 mm x 12 m long
- ✔ Geotextile liner: 36 sq metres
- ✔ Duct tape
- ✔ Butyl: 1 piece 10 m x 1.8 m
- ✔ Concrete: 1 part cement (120 kg) and 4 parts ballast (480 kg)
- ✔ Mortar: 1 part cement (40 kg) and 3 parts sand (120 kg)
- ✔ Stones: 1 cu metre
- ✔ Land drainage pipe: 2 m long
- ✔ Submersible pump
- ✔ Mastic

Tools

- ✔ Tape measure and spray marker
- ✔ Spade, fork and shovel
- ✔ Hacksaw
- ✔ Scissors
- ✔ Bricklayer's trowel

Cut-away view of the planted stream

A "collar" of stones

Stones
Set in a
mortar bed

Concrete at
the edge
reinforces
the sides

**Small stones and
shards of rock**

Stones
placed to create
pools and water
movements

**Buried
armoured
electric cable**

Submersible pump

Boggy area
Perforated land drain
prevents the water from
becoming stagnant

Concrete
50 mm thick

Stones placed on
edge of geotextile
during construction

Geotextile

Butyl
The sides need to be
at least 100 mm higher
than the water level

Geotextile

Delivery pipe
50 mm diameter.
Buried in the base
of the excavation

Boggy area
Use clay loam
for this area

Edge of the stream
disguised with plants
and rocks

Rocks hide the point
at which the lined
stream begins

Delivery pipe
Above water
level and
concealed by
a rock

Pond
Provides water
for the stream

Making the planted stream

1 Excavating
Dig out the entire area to a depth 100 mm below the projected stream bed. Put in the 50 mm flexible pipe which will deliver the water from the pump to the source, and bury it in the base of the excavation.

2 Laying the liner
Remove any sharp objects from the bed of the excavation, then cover with a layer of geotextile, securing any joins with duct tape. Line the stream area with butyl, ensuring that at least 100 mm remains above the predicted water level where the stream will run.

3 Spreading the concrete base
Cover the lined area with another layer of geotextile followed by a 50 mm thick layer of concrete. Do not worry too much about creating a perfectly smooth finish as stones will cover most of the area. Leave to cure overnight.

4 Sculpting the watercourse
Lay down a mortar bed, shaping the watercourse as required and covering the stream bed with stones before the mortar has cured. A clay loam is ideal for the bog garden area. For a natural look, use one type of rock. In the boggy areas, perforated land drain should be placed in the deepest part to stop the water from becoming stagnant.

5 Installing the pump
Make sure the delivery pipe is above water level and disguise it with a one or more rocks. Attach a submersible pump and an adjustable valve to the lower end of the pipe and immerse it in the pond. Run the stream at the maximum possible ensuring there is no spillage over the sides of the butyl.

6 Trimming and finishing
Cut away any excess geotextile and butyl, covering the edge with earth or stones and hiding the point where the lined stream begins. Reduce the water flow to the desired pace and plant the bog areas. If you modify the stream at a later date check the liner sides again!

Kidney-shaped pond

Because the size and shape of this project are easily adjustable this pond can fit most gardens. The smart brick edging allows you to walk around the pond throughout the year without getting muddy or wet shoes and it could easily fit into a patio scheme or be surrounded by grass, gravel or a sweeping brick path. When you mark out the organic kidney shape try to avoid it getting too narrow at any point.

★
Easy

**Making time
6 weekends**
*Three days for
excavating the hole
and the remaining
time to complete*

Overall dimensions and general notes

*Make sure that the size of
the pond does not interfere
with access to the garden.*

*The depth of the water will
be affected by the shape of
the pond; do not make it too
narrow at any point*

5.3 m long

3.5 m wide

*Look for bricks
that match the
house so the
pond blends in*

You will need

Materials

- ✔ Geotextile: 54 sq metre
- ✔ Duct tape
- ✔ Butyl sheet: 1 piece 7.8 m x 6 m
- ✔ Concrete: 1 part cement (180 kg) and 4 parts ballast (720 kg)
- ✔ Mortar: 1 part cement (40 kg) and 3 parts sand (120 kg)
- ✔ Bricks: 210 for the retaining walls and 120 for the coping
- ✔ Sand: 350 kg

Tools

- ✔ Tape measure, 15 m long hosepipe (for marking shape), spray marker and peg
- ✔ Spirit level
- ✔ Club hammer
- ✔ Spade, fork and shovel
- ✔ Scissors
- ✔ Bricklayer's trowel
- ✔ Pointing trowel

Considering the design

This pond can be shaped to suit the garden where a formal or geometric shaped pond is not required. The edges can be marked out with a garden hose, and viewed from all sides before the final shape is chosen. Remember that the further away from a round shape that the pond finally forms, the more difficult it will be to get an adequate depth of water. Deep water will, in the long term, reduce maintenance requirements and aid the pond's ecology, reducing blanketweed, for example. Never leave children unsupervised near a pond.

Getting started

Trim back or remove any existing plants that may be affected by the works. Consider what you are going to do with the spoil, how you are going to move it and by what route and tell your neighbours about your plans. Assemble your materials and equipment. Choose a dry day but make sure that you have somewhere to store your cement (off the ground and covered with waterproof material) should it suddenly rain while the work is in progress. Remember the final shape and depth of your pond will alter the quantities given above.

Cut-away detail of the kidney-shaped pond

Planting shelf
Cover with a clay loam mixture

Marginal plant

Brick wall

Coping brick
Choose good-quality bricks that have a pleasant colour

Geotextile

Surrounding area can be gravel, bricks or grass

Butyl

1 in 3 gradient

Mortar

Brick edge to planting shelf

Sand
Sharp sand is used to fill the cavity

Mortar

Soil

Geotextile

Concrete footings
300 mm x 100 mm

Butyl

Geotextile

Exploded view of the kidney-shaped pond

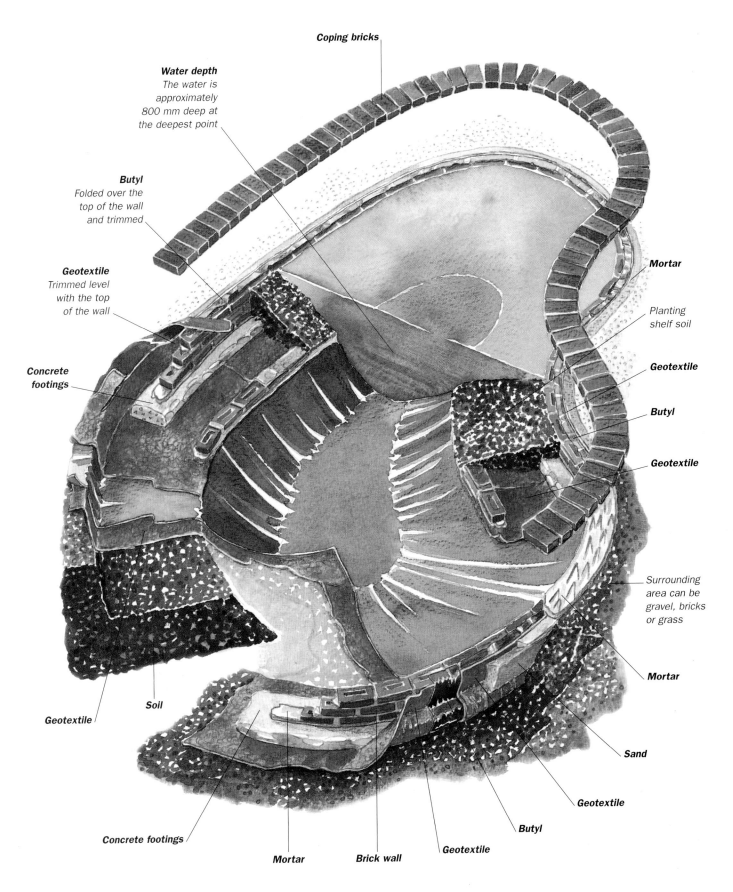

Coping bricks

Water depth
The water is approximately 800 mm deep at the deepest point

Butyl
Folded over the top of the wall and trimmed

Geotextile
Trimmed level with the top of the wall

Concrete footings

Geotextile

Soil

Concrete footings

Mortar

Brick wall

Geotextile

Mortar

Planting shelf soil

Geotextile

Butyl

Geotextile

Surrounding area can be gravel, bricks or grass

Mortar

Sand

Geotextile

Butyl

Making the kidney-shaped pond

1 Setting out the pond
Clearly mark out the area of the pond plus 300 mm all round, marking the intended water level with a peg set outside the working area. Dig the entire area, to a level depth of 300 mm. Mark the final shape of the pond, using marker spray on the levelled ground.

2 Digging out the pond
Where planting shelves are to be built into the sides of the pond, mark out where you want them to be. Dig out the central area of the pond allowing for a 1 in 3 gradient from the marked areas. Remove any sharp stones.

3 Lining the excavation with geotextile
Unroll the geotextile (which usually comes in 2 m wide rolls) to cover the entire excavation allowing 100 mm overlaps. Using short lengths of duct tape join the sides of the geotextile together at 1 m intervals.

4 Lining the excavation with butyl
Make sure that no stones or sharp objects have fallen into the excavation, unroll the butyl liner and spread it ensuring that there is at least 300 mm of liner overlapping the edge of the pond all around. Avoid treading on the liner but take off your boots if you have to.

5 Protecting the liner
Where the liner will come into direct contact with the concrete footings or brick-built sides of the pond, cover it with a further layer of geotextile, being careful that no stones or other objects come between the liner and the geotextile.

6 Building the footings and edges
On the flat ledge within the excavation, build a concrete footing 100 mm deep by 300 mm wide, making sure it is flat and level. Smooth the sides with a finishing trowel and leave to cure overnight. Build up the interior edge to the pond with three courses of bricks.

7 Filling the cavity
Gently fold the liner and geotextile over the top of the brick edging and fill the cavity between the wall and the earth with sharp sand. Compact the sand with your feet to avoid later subsidence. Do not try compacting the sand with sharp tools.

8 Preparing the planting shelves
Where the level shelf has been extended into the pond to create a planting shelf, lay a single course of bricks bedded in mortar to keep the soil from falling into the bottom of the pond. Fill the planting area with soil – a clay loam mixture is ideal.

9 Trimming the lining
Cut away the visible edges of the geotextile (any that pokes above the bricks). Leave 50 mm of butyl above the bricks and cut off the remainder. Lay this on top of the bricks.

10 Laying the coping bricks
Lay the brick edging on a bed of mortar. Ensure that you trap the butyl between the bricks and maintain even-looking gaps all around. Allow the mortar to dry for a few days before filling with water.

Circular pond

Intermediate

Making time
3 weekends
*A weekend for
digging the hole and
two weekends to
complete*

Filled with submerged and floating-leaved plants and their attendant wildlife, this unobtrusive, classical shape adds wonderful mirror reflections as well as beauty and interest on both the surface of the water and below it. The paved surround is perfect for sitting on when the sun is out and allows easy access to the pond, especially when the time comes to do some maintenance work on it.

Considering the design

You may wish to build this pond as part of a patio using matching stone pavers, or it could simply stand alone where it has the appearance of a well. As with all pond projects, consider the safety of children at all times (see page 13).

Getting started

Once you have chosen a level site, mark it out with pegs and string and "live with it" for a few days so that you can be sure it is in the best place for your garden. Try to complete the excavation and lining quickly, as the unsupported sides will start to collapse if there is rain during its construction.

Overall dimensions and general notes

2.78 m square

Ideal for a small formal garden, this circular pond would look good either as an extension to an existing patio or set in a lawn. You could use real stone crazy paving or bricks for the surround.

The pond is 1.5 m in diameter and is surrounded by a reconstituted stone paving kit

You will need

Materials

- Paving kit: 38 mm thick pavers forming a 2.78 m square with a 1.5 m diameter hole in the middle
- Geotextile: 37 sq metres
- Butyl liner: 1 piece 4.3 m square
- Wood: 1 piece 1.9 m x 90 mm x 60 mm and 2 pieces 1.2 m x 90 mm x 30 mm (tamping beam), 1 piece 200 mm x 75 mm x 75 mm and 1 piece 1.1 m x 35 mm x 25 mm (tramel), and 1 piece 1.84 m x 90 mm x 30 mm (beam for checking level)
- Plywood: 1 piece 500 mm square

- Nails: 5 at 60 mm long
- Concrete: 1 part cement (72 kg), and 4 parts ballast (288 kg)
- Bricks: 220
- Mortar: 1 part cement (50 kg) and 3 parts sand (150 kg)
- Builders sand: 1500 kg
- Hardcore: 0.5 cu metre

Tools

- Pegs and string
- Club hammer
- Tape measure and spray marker

- Spade, fork and shovel
- Wheelbarrow and bucket
- Scissors
- General-purpose saw
- Claw hammer
- Bricklayer's towel
- Pointing towel
- Spirit level
- Sledgehammer

Cross-section of the circular pond

Sand
50 mm thick

Maximum water level

1.64 m diameter

Paving slab
38 mm thick

Hardcore
50 mm thick

788 mm deep

Lining
A layer of geotextile, followed by butyl, followed by geotextile

Earth

Concrete foundation
65 mm thick

Sand
Fills the cavity between the liner and the earth. Poured in after the brick wall is completed

Sand
10–20 mm thick

Cut-away plan view of the circular pond

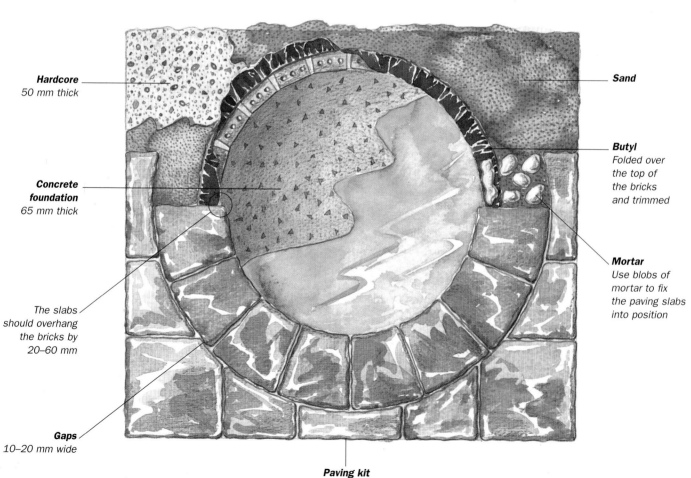

Hardcore
50 mm thick

Sand

Concrete foundation
65 mm thick

Butyl
Folded over the top of the bricks and trimmed

Mortar
Use blobs of mortar to fix the paving slabs into position

The slabs should overhang the bricks by 20–60 mm

Gaps
10–20 mm wide

Paving kit
Approximately 2.78 m square with a 1.5 m diameter circular hole

Exploded view of the circular pond

Paving kit
Approximately 2.78 m square
with a 1.5 m diameter circular hole

Sand
50 mm thick.
Firmly compacted

Hardcore
50 mm thick.
Firmly compacted

1.5 m in diameter

Paving kit
Available in different designs

Gaps
10–20 mm wide.
Fill with quite dry
mortar (mortar
mixed with a small
quantity of water)

Bricks
10 courses of bricks.
Aim for 10 mm-thick
courses

Geotextile

Butyl

Geotextile

Sand
10–20 mm thick

Concrete foundation
65 mm thick

Making the circular pond

1 Setting out the slabs
Set the paving slabs down and try them for position. Live with them for a few days. Check the dimensions of the whole square and the diameter of the circle as kits may vary slightly in size. Aim for the slabs to overhang the brick walls of the pond by 20–60 mm.

2 Marking the area
Use a tape measure, pegs, string and a spray marker to draw a circle 2 m in diameter. If your earth is crumbly it can be difficult to dig an accurately-sized hole so start by marking out a larger circle – one 2.6 m in diameter, for example.

3 Excavating the hole
Remove the turf with the spade and fork and start digging. You may wish to save the topsoil for another area of the garden and discard the rest. Make a hole 2 m in diameter and 860 mm deep, making sure it is clean-sided.

4 Lining with geotextile
Remove all sharp stones and spread a 10–20 mm layer of sand over the bottom of the hole. Cover the base and sides of the hole with geotextile, allowing for generous overlaps of at least 100 mm. Leave it overlapping until step 11.

5 Lining with butyl
Cover the geotextile with the 4.3 m square sheet of butyl. You will find this easier if you have someone to help. Take time arranging the creases so that they end up evenly distributed and weigh down the edges with bricks. Do not put any water in at this stage.

6 Laying the concrete slab
Reline the hole with geotextile (this protects the top side of the butyl) and weigh that down with bricks. Lay a 65 mm thick slab of concrete in the hole. Use the saw and nails to build the tamping beam and ask someone to hold the other end while you work.

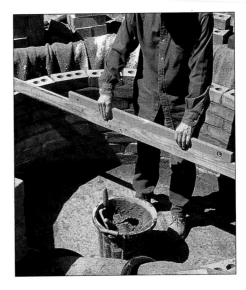

7 Using the trammel

Use the plywood, stick, block, and nails to make a trammel (this works like the minute hand on a clock) that scribes a radius of 820 mm. Centre the trammel on the concrete base, weigh it down with bricks, and use it to indicate the correct position of each brick.

8 Building the wall

Build the circular wall with 10 mm thick mortar joints and stagger each course as shown. After completing each course, you can continue using the trammel by raising it upward by 75 mm each time, or you can simply check the brickwork is vertical using a spirit level.

9 Checking the levels

Check the level every two courses using the 1.84 m long piece of wood and the spirit level. Bear in mind that the pond must be completely level otherwise it will not look right. Continue building until you have completed the 10 courses.

10 Packing with sand

Use sand to fill any spaces between the sides of the hole and the geotextile. Dig out the surrounding earth down to a depth of 100 mm below the bricks. Spread 50 mm of hardcore and make sure that it is firmly compacted using the sledgehammer.

11 Trimming the lining

Pack the top of the cavity with concrete. Cut the geotextile off level with the bricks. Flap the butyl over the top of the wall and trim off the excess.

12 Putting down the paving

Spread a 50 mm layer of sand over the hardcore and compact this so it finishes level with the top of the bricks. Bed the paving slabs on blobs of mortar and when that has set, fill the joints with a quite dry mortar (mixed with less water so that it is still crumbly).

Formal canal

This beautiful design by John Brookes is part of a formal arrangement and takes the formality of the house out into the garden. It is both simple and classic and the long strip of still water reflects the sky. The brickwork edge finishes flush with the surrounding brick, gravel and lawn, making it smart and practical. This design is easy to reduce down in size for a smaller garden or courtyard.

★★
Intermediate

Making time
4 weekends
2 weekends for making the foundation and 2 weekends to complete

Considering the design

As with any formal water feature, the most important thing is to make the scheme fit the environment, so make sure that your canal allows for easy access to all areas of the garden and does not act as a "moat" to discourage use of parts of the garden. Where young children are about it is dangerous as they may crawl or walk into the canal and not be able climb out. If you have young children it is better to wait a few years for them to grow up before building a pond or if you are expecting children to visit you may consider putting up some form of temporary barrier (see page 13). In order for the water plants to flourish it is important that the depth of water is not reduced below 600 mm. It is important that the water level and the level of the patio are carefully considered so that no more steps than are necessary from the house to the pond are incorporated in the design, which is elegant and requires little maintenance.

Getting started

At nearly 5 m long this is a big excavation so you do need to consider where you are going to put the spoil. You could pay to have it removed or why not plan a rockery or other feature that requires a quantity of soil?

Overall dimensions and general notes

4.94 m long

1.49 m wide

This canal is suited to classic still water plants, such as water lilies.

You will need

Materials

- Hardcore: 0.7 cu metres
- Wood: 26 metres of 100 mm x 20 mm section (foundation frame and tamping pieces), 26 pieces 300 mm x 35 mm x 20 mm (foundation frame pegs)
- Plywood: 1 piece 500 mm square x 13 mm (general use)
- Nails: 34 at 38 mm long
- Concrete: 1 part cement (650 kg) and 4 parts (2600 kg) ballast
- Blocks: 143
- Bricks: 183 for the walls and 160 for the coping
- Mortar: 1 part (90 kg) cement and 3 parts (270 kg) sand
- Geotextile: 60 sq metre
- Duct tape
- Butyl: 1 piece 7.5 m x 4 m

Tools

- Tape measure, pegs, string, and a piece of chalk
- Club hammer
- Spade, fork and shovel
- Sledgehammer
- General-purpose saw
- Claw hammer
- Spirit level
- Line set
- Bricklayer's trowel
- Pointing trowel

Cut-away detail of the formal canal

Surrounding surface is optional

Coping bricks

Geotextile

Butyl

Geotextile

Sand infil

Mortar joints

Concrete slab
Forms the bottom of the pond

Concrete foundation

Hardcore

Soil

Cross-section detail of the formal canal

Water level

Coping brick

Outer wall
Blocks and bricks

Inner walls
Blocks and bricks

Sand

Concrete slab
140 mm thick

10 mm mortar joints

Cavity
Approximately 33 mm wide

Trench
390 mm wide and 300 mm deep

Pond lining
Geotextile / butyl / geotextile layers (approximately 10–30 mm)

Concrete
150 mm thick

Hardcore
150 mm thick

Exploded view of the formal canal (coping bricks not shown)

Two courses of bricks

Inner wall

Two courses of blocks

Geotextile
*Trimmed level
with the top
of the walls*

Butyl
*Overlaps the
top of the
exterior wall*

Geotextile
*Trimmed level
with the top
of the walls*

Concrete slab
*140 mm thick
forms the bottom
of the pond*

Sand
*Used to fill
the cavity
between the
wall and
earth once
the pond
is built*

Exterior wall

Single course
of bricks

Three courses
of blocks

Earth

Hardcore
150 mm thick

Concrete foundation
150 mm thick

Making the formal canal

1 Excavating the area
Clearly mark out an area 5.1 m x 1.7 m and remove all materials in it to a depth of 863 mm. Mark out a 390 mm-wide foundation trench into the bottom of the hole and remove the earth to a depth of 300 mm.

2 Laying the foundation
Fill the trench with hardcore to a depth of 150 mm. Use pegs and wood to form a level frame and fill this with concrete. Tamp the concrete level with the frame using a piece of spare wood. Leave to set overnight.

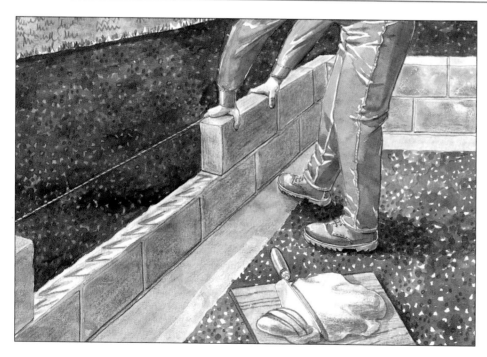

3 Building the exterior wall
Remove the wood frame and mark out the position of the outside edge of the exterior wall on the concrete using the chalk (4.99 m x 1.54 m).

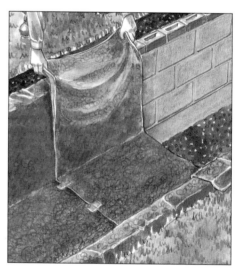

4 Lining with geotextile
Carefully line the entire area with geotextile right to the top, folding or cutting away the darts that are formed at the corners. Use duct tape to join the pieces together.

5 Lining with butyl
Place the butyl liner into the lined area, ensuring the sides reach the top all round. Use bricks wrapped in geotextile to push the liner into the corners, fold and tape the darts that rise from each corner. Cut away the liner 100 mm above the top of the bricks.

6 Laying the concrete slab
Reline the hole with more geotextile. Make a tamping frame from the spare wood and use it to cover the bottom of the hole with a level layer of concrete about 140 mm deep. Allow to dry overnight.

7 Building the inner wall
Use the chalk to mark out the inside edge of the inner wall (4.5 m x 1.06 m). This leaves a cavity of about 33 mm to accomodate the lining. Build up two courses of blocks followed by two courses of bricks.

8 Putting on the coping bricks
Trim the geotextile layers level with the top of the cavity wall and weigh down the butyl so that it overlaps the top of the exterior wall. Lay coping bricks on a bed of mortar and finish by filling the cavity between the wall and the earth with sand.

Pond with bridge and beach

An informal wildlife pond provides interest all year round and fascinates children and adults alike. A wide range of pond life quickly grows up and newts, frogs and toads often appear as if by magic. A natural-looking beach and imaginative planting with lilies, iris and primroses complete the picture. The simple plank bridge gives a sense of adventure and can also save you walking all the way around the pond!

★★
Intermediate

**Making time
4 weekends**
2 weekends for digging the hole and 2 weekends for finishing

Overall dimensions and general notes

A 4 m long bridge spans the narrowest point of the pond

The best all-round advice is to go for the biggest pond that money, time and space allows.

The pond is approximately 8 m long and 5 m wide

An area of natural-looking beach

Considering the design

This pond can be built anywhere in the garden and is often away from the house in a quiet spot with wild flower and native species planting. It is often appropriate to put a bench or seat nearby for quiet contemplation. Be sure to make it as large as possible as plant growth on the water will soon make it appear smaller than it actually is. Make sure that you leave a clear area on one side so that you can walk up to it and see it clearly. People will be drawn to it if they can see a reflection or shimmer from the house. A pebble "beach" provides an attractive edge to the pond (see inset). As always, consider child safety (see page 13).

Getting started

See if you can find a place to put the earth from the excavations elsewhere in the garden (build a rockery for example), as this can be expensive to remove.

You will need

Materials

- Geotextile: 115 sq metres
- Duct tape
- Butyl: 1 piece 11 m x 8 m
- Concrete: 1 part cement (450 kg) and 4 parts ballast (1800 kg)
- Bricks: 315
- Mortar: 1 part cement (50 kg) and 3 parts sand (150 kg)
- Wood: 3 pieces, 490 mm x 100 mm x 100 mm (bridge frame horizontals), 6 pieces 700 mm x 100 mm x 100 mm (bridge frame verticals), 2 pieces (natural irregular edge is optional) 4 m x 250–300 mm x 50 mm (bridge planks)
- Bolts: 12 at 180 mm x M12 each with 1 nut and 2 washers, galvanised (bridge frames)
- Nails: 12 at 130 mm long, galvanised flat headed
- Plywood: 1.22 m x 600 mm x 26 mm (general work board)
- Sand: 700 kg

Tools

- Tape measure, hosepipe or rope (30 m long, for marking pond shape), spray marker and peg
- Club hammer and claw hammer
- Spade, fork and shovel
- Wheelbarrow and bucket
- Spirit level
- Rake
- Scissors
- Bricklayer's trowel and pointing trowel
- General-purpose saw
- Drill and 12 mm diameter bit

Cross-section detail of the bridge

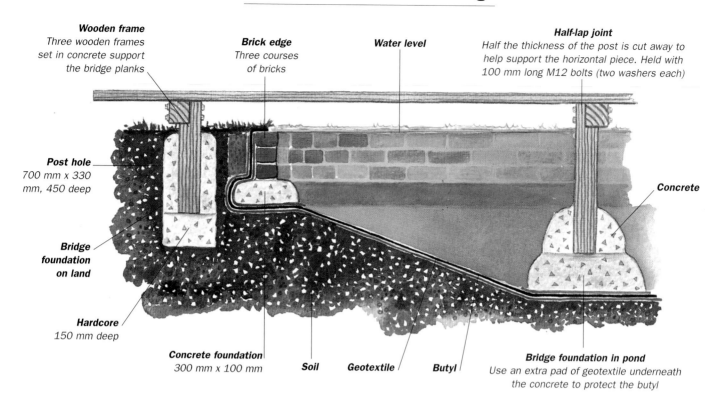

Wooden frame
Three wooden frames set in concrete support the bridge planks

Brick edge
Three courses of bricks

Water level

Half-lap joint
Half the thickness of the post is cut away to help support the horizontal piece. Held with 100 mm long M12 bolts (two washers each)

Post hole
700 mm x 330 mm, 450 deep

Bridge foundation on land

Concrete

Hardcore
150 mm deep

Concrete foundation
300 mm x 100 mm

Soil

Geotextile

Butyl

Bridge foundation in pond
Use an extra pad of geotextile underneath the concrete to protect the butyl

Cross-section detail of the pond showing beach (bridge not shown)

Planting shelf

Sand infill

Brick edge

Water
1.1 m deep at the deepest point

Brick edge to planting shelf and beach

Beach

Brick edge

Concrete foundation

Extra layer of geotextile under shelf and beach areas

Geotextile

Soil

Butyl

Bottom of pond

Geotextile

Planting shelf

Exploded view of the pond with bridge and beach

Sand
Fill cavity between wall and earth with sand

Bridge planks
2 pieces 4 m x
250–300 mm x 50 mm.
Fixed to the bridge
frames with 130 mm nails

Bridge frame
1 piece, 490 mm x 100 mm x 100 mm
(bridge frame horizontal) and 2 pieces 700 mm x
100 mm x 100 mm (bridge frame verticals)

Brick edging to
planting shelf

Planting shelf
Filled with clay
loam for planting
marginal plants

**Bridge foundation
on land**

There is an extra
layer of geotextile
over the shelf
and beach areas

Geotextile
Trim level with
top of bricks

Beach shelf
Filled with shingle and
pebbles to imitate a beach

Geotextile

Butyl
Overlapping
bricks and
trimmed to shape

Foundation for
the brick edge

Making the pond with bridge and beach

1 Excavating the area
Mark out the area of the pond. Near the pond but outside the workings drive in a wooden marker peg so the top is at the intended water level. Dig the area to 300 mm below that level and mark out planting shelf areas. Dig out the remaining earth to finish the hole.

2 Measuring and raking
Allow at least 300 mm extra on both length and width. Rake over the excavation removing any sharp objects which could damage the liner.

3 Lining the excavation
Cover the entire excavation with geotextile, allowing for 100 mm overlaps. Spread the butyl over the geotextile ensuring that it extends beyond the water level all round when the pond is filled. Rearrange creases so that they are distributed evenly.

4 Laying extra geotextile
Make sure that no stones or sharp objects have fallen into the excavation and then lay extra geotextile over the planting shelf and beach areas. Use short lengths of duct tape to join the 1 m wide sheets of geotextile.

5 Building the footings and edges
On the flat ledge within the excavation build a concrete footing 100 mm deep by 300 mm wide, ensuring it is level and flat. Smooth all the sides with a finishing trowel and leave to cure overnight. Build up the interior edge to the pond with 3 courses of bricks.

6 Building the bridge frames
Establish the finished height of your bridge and prepare the bridge frame components accordingly. Mould a concrete pad for supporting the central frame. Hold it upright while you spread a mound of concrete around the bottoms of the wooden posts.

7 Completing the bridge

Dig holes either side of the pond and set the other two frames in concrete so that they are vertical and also levelled and aligned with the central frame. Once the concrete has set, fix the bridge planks to the tops of the frames using nails.

8 Backfilling behind the lining

The geotextile needs to be trimmed level with the top of the bricks and the butyl should overlap the bricks and then be trimmed. Fill the cavity behind the wall with sand. Compact the sand with your feet to avoid later subsidence but take care to avoid damaging the liner.

9 Preparing the planting shelves

Where the level shelf has been extended into the pond to create a planting shelf, check that you have adequate geotextile protecting the butyl and then lay a line of bricks along the edge (mortar is not required). Fill the planting shelves with clay loam.

10 Creating the beach and finishing the pond

Fill the beach area with a mixture of shingle and differently sized pebbles. Use a board to protect the edge of the pond while you work. When the pond is filled with water, cover the tops of the bricks with turf, cutting the turf at the edge of the water. Alternatively, cover with soil and sow grass seed.

Raised pond

Ideal for a small garden or patio area, the coping allows for seating close to the water where you can see into the water as well as looking at the reflections of the sky and seasons. It is adaptable and takes up little space and, where there are children around it is safer, as they are less likely to stumble into the water. Placed where it can be seen from the house, it will give interest and delight throughout the year.

★ ★
Intermediate

Making time
4 weekends
A weekend to make the foundation and 3 weekends for completion

Considering the design

This little pond can be square or rectangular in shape and should be as large as possible, allowing for access around the area. The coping stone is 526 mm above the ground and this is just about low enough to make a comfortable seating place. Place it where it can be seen from inside the house from a much-used vantage point. Use materials that closely match those that form your house. Consider the reflections that you will see from your vantage point; placing a mirror (horizontally) where the water level will ultimately be will give you a good idea of the end result. Consider any services (water, drainage, TV, electricity, gas, or sewerage) that may be underneath the proposed site and alter the scheme accordingly. Note how the pond butts against the wall; a good option if you are short of space.

Getting started

Make a drawing showing the size that you have chosen. Use this to order the material that you will want. Allow 10% over on all materials. If materials have to be carried through the house remove or protect vulnerable things.

You will need

Materials

✔ Concrete: 1 part cement (30 kg) and 4 parts ballast (120 kg)

✔ Wood: 1.5 m x 70 mm x 30 mm (tamping beam)

✔ Bricks: 196 bricks and 180 handmade irregular bricks (approximately 228 mm x 102.5 mm x 67 mm)

✔ Mortar mix: 1 part cement (75 kg) and 3 parts sand (225 kg)

✔ Plywood: 1.22 m x 610 mm x 9 mm (general workboard)

✔ Rigid liner: 1.8 m x 1.3 m (at outer rim) and 508 mm deep

✔ Stone slabs: 22 tiles, 295 mm square and 35 mm thick

Tools

✔ Tape measure, pegs, string and a piece of chalk

✔ Club hammer

✔ Spade, fork and shovel

✔ Wheelbarrow and bucket

✔ Spirit level

✔ Line set

✔ Bricklayer's trowel and pointing trowel

✔ Angle grinder

Overall dimensions and general notes

The edge of the pond is ideal for sitting on

Ideal for fish and plants or you could install a fountain and statuette

526 mm high

1.756 m wide

2.22 m long

This pond structure is built around a pre-formed rigid liner, so purchase the liner to suit your space first, and then adjust the material quantities accordingly.

Plan view of the raised pond showing first courses of brick wall

The double wall forms a strong structure and a suitably wide support for the top slabs

Inner wall
Metric bricks
(215 mm x
102.5 mm x
65 mm)

Outer wall
Handmade
irregular bricks
(Approximately 228 mm
x 102.5 mm x 67 mm)

Concrete
2.2 m x 1.741 m
300 mm wide
120 mm thick

Gap
The gap between
the walls can be
adjusted from
0–15 mm to
compensate for
irregular sizes of
brick and uneven
mortar gaps

Cross-section of the raised pond

50 mm overhang
all around

Planting shelf

Slabs
Centred on walls

Concrete
300 mm wide
120 mm thick

Sand

Walls need to
be centred on
foundation

Exploded view of the raised pond

Slabs
295 mm square
35 mm thick
Total of 22 required

*Slabs cut to fit
(the two smallest
pieces are cut
from 1 slab)

Inner wall
1.887 m x 1.44 m
28 metric bricks per course
7 courses
Total 196

Rigid liner
1.8 m x 1.3 m
508 mm deep
(external measurements
including the rim around
the top edge)

Outer wall
2.119 m x 1.656 m
30 Handmade irregular
bricks per course
6 courses
Total 180

Sand

Concrete
2.2 m x 1.741 m
300 mm wide
120 mm thick
30 mm below ground level

Lawn or
patio surround

Making the raised pond

1 Marking out
Using the tape measure, pegs and string, set out the shape of the foundation on the grass – 2.2 m long and 1.741 mm wide. Remove the turf.

2 Positioning the levelling pegs
Dig out the foundation trench, 300 mm wide and 150 mm deep. Hammer in a series of wooden pegs to establish a level about 30 mm lower than the lawn.

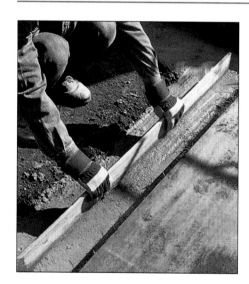

3 Tamping the concrete
Fill the foundation trench with concrete up to the level of the wooden pegs. (Note the workboard to protect the lawn.)

4 Practise laying the bricks
Set out the first course of bricks without using mortar so that you can see how the pattern works. Arrange the ordinary bricks on the inside and the larger handmade bricks on the outside. Try to avoid cutting bricks.

5 Building the walls
Build up the inside walls to a height of six courses, and check both the vertical and horizontal levels. Use the line set to help you lay the bricks in accurate straight lines.

6 Fitting the rigid liner

Sit the plastic liner in the brick box so that the rim is resting on top of the wall. Fill the cavity between the liner and the wall with sand. Avoid leaving any gaps as these can cause the liner to distort or break over time (see page 26).

7 Cleaning the mortar joints

Build up the outside wall at the corners so that the top course is slightly higher than the level of the inner wall. Use the handle of the trowel to rake the courses to a clean finish while the mortar is still workable.

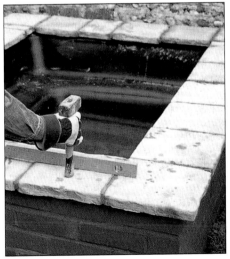

8 Finishing the brickwork

Continue laying up the courses until you have finished the exterior wall. Keep checking with the spirit level and making adjustments as necessary.

9 Laying the coping slabs

Practice arranging the slabs around the top of the pond allowing for a 50 mm overhang all around. Try to avoid cutting slabs where possible. Trowel a generous layer of mortar on top of the walls and bed the coping slabs in place. Check that they are level.

Pond with decking

Decking over a pond invites you to step over the water on to a different world. To look down in the gaps between the boards adds to the sense of adventure like being on a pleasure pier, a boat or raft. A railing is a good idea – made from metal or wood – and will stop young children falling in and will give you somewhere to rest your elbows and feel secure while looking down into the pond and observing the wildlife.

★ ★ ★
Advanced

Making time
4 weekends
A weekend for digging the hole and 2 weekends for construction

Considering the design

Decking can disguise the point at which the land stops and the pond starts so this combination has a lot of potential. You can alter the size and shape of the deck-ing to suit your requirements.

The deck boards need to be strong and resistant to rotting. Preserved pine (stained or painted) is suitable but untreated bare oak is even better. If you have railings, they need to be strong, well supported and about 1 m high.

Getting started

If you require a deck of a different size and shape or are working with an existing pond, start by planning it out on paper.

Overall dimensions and general notes

Decking boards made from preserved pine or bare oak

An irregular shaped pond with a natural-looking edge, 5.3 m x 3.5 m

2.27 m wide

3.356 m long

The size and shape of the decking can be altered to suit your needs but be sure to provide adequate supports. Wood or metal railing is a sensible option.

You will need

Materials

- ✔ Geotextile: 54 sq metres
- ✔ Duct tape
- ✔ Butyl: 1 piece 7 m x 6 m
- ✔ Concrete: 1 part cement (225 kg) and 4 parts (900 kg) ballast
- ✔ Bricks: 210
- ✔ Mortar: 1 part cement (38 kg) and 3 parts sand (114 kg)
- ✔ Sand: 400 kg
- ✔ Hardcore: 0.1 cu metre
- ✔ Tanking paint: 5 litres

- ✔ Wood: 10 pieces, 350 mm x 100 mm x 100 mm (posts), 2 pieces 2.2 m x 100 mm x 100 mm (deck frame horizontals, long), 2 pieces 1.2 m x 100 mm x 100 mm (deck frame horizontals, short), 6 pieces 3.356 m x 200 mm x 50 mm (deck boards, long) and 5 pieces 1.364 m x 200 mm x 50 mm (deck boards, short)
- ✔ Plywood: 1.5 m x 50 mm x 6–7 mm (strip to set deck board gaps)
- ✔ Bolts: 20 at 180 mm x M12 each with 1 nut and 2 washers, galvanised
- ✔ Nails: 68 at 130 mm long, galvanised

Tools

- ✔ Tape measure, 20 m of rope or hosepipe (for marking shape of pond), peg and spray marker
- ✔ Spade, fork and shovel
- ✔ Spirit level
- ✔ Scissors
- ✔ Bricklayer's trowel and pointing trowel
- ✔ General-purpose saw
- ✔ Spanner (to fit nuts)
- ✔ Claw hammer

Exploded view of the pond with decking

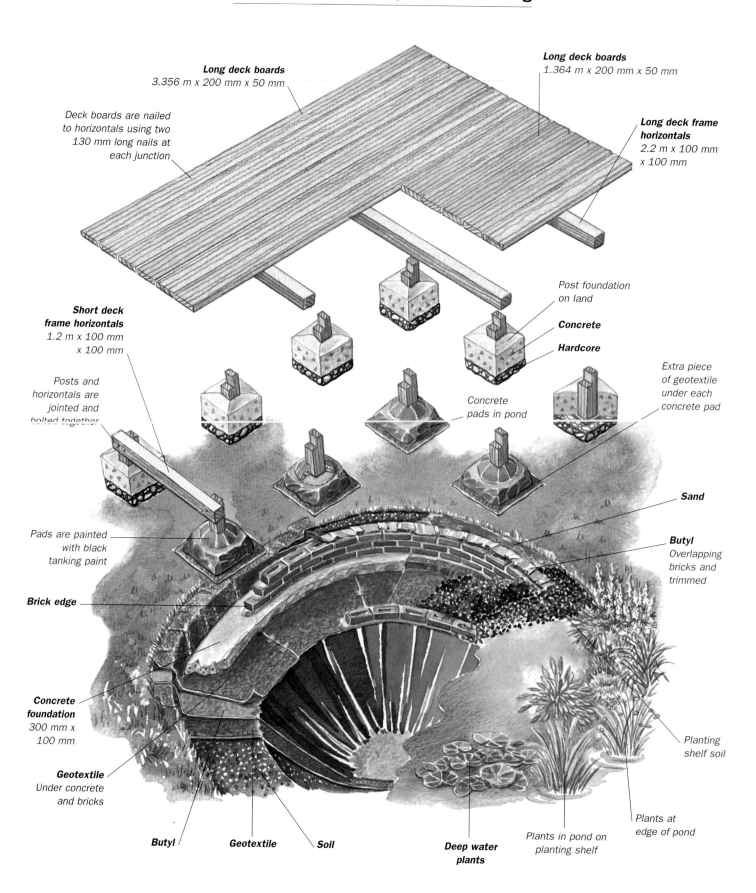

Long deck boards
3.356 m x 200 mm x 50 mm

Long deck boards
1.364 m x 200 mm x 50 mm

Deck boards are nailed to horizontals using two 130 mm long nails at each junction

Long deck frame horizontals
2.2 m x 100 mm x 100 mm

Short deck frame horizontals
1.2 m x 100 mm x 100 mm

Posts and horizontals are jointed and bolted together

Post foundation on land

Concrete

Hardcore

Concrete pads in pond

Extra piece of geotextile under each concrete pad

Pads are painted with black tanking paint

Sand

Butyl
Overlapping bricks and trimmed

Brick edge

Concrete foundation
300 mm x 100 mm

Geotextile
Under concrete and bricks

Butyl   **Geotextile**   **Soil**

Deep water plants

Plants in pond on planting shelf

Plants at edge of pond

Planting shelf soil

Cut-away detail of the pond with decking

Butyl
Folded over brick edge and trimmed

Edge of excavation

Sand
Fill cavity between earth and wall with sand

Deck boards
200 mm x 50 mm in section.
Fixed with two 130 mm long nails at each junction

Trim geotextile level with top of wall

Half-lap joint
A piece 100 mm x 100 mm x 50 mm is cut from the post

Post
Set in a hole 350 mm square and 300 mm deep

Butyl

Nut and bolt
Two 180 mm long M12 bolt are used at each joint with a washer each side

Mortar
Spread around bottoms of posts

Concrete pad
Approximately 350 mm square and 150 mm high

Extra geotextile under pad

Soil

Geotextile

Concrete

Hardcore
75 mm thick

Edge of excavation

Concrete foundation for brick edge

Geotextile

Butyl

Making the pond with decking

1 Marking out and excavating
Clearly mark out the area of the pond plus 300 mm all round and dig to a depth of 350 mm. Mark out the final shape of the pond. Where planting shelves are to be built in to the sides of the pond, mark out the shelves and then finish digging out the pond.

2 Lining the pond
Remove any sharp objects from the hole. Cover the entire excavation with geotextile allowing 100 mm overlaps. Use duct tape to join the sides together at 1 m intervals. Unroll the butyl liner and lay it over the area, ensuring it extends beyond the intended water level.

3 Building the footing
Protect the liner with another layer of geotextile on the shelf areas. On the flat ledge within the excavation build a concrete footing 100 mm deep by 300 mm wide ensuring it is level and flat. Smooth all the sides with a finishing trowel and leave to cure overnight.

5 Making the planting shelves
Fill the area behind the wall with sand, compact it with your feet to avoid later subsidence and trim the geotextile and butyl. Lay bricks along the edge of the planting shelves and fill these recesses with soil for planting.

4 Building the edges
Build the interior edge to the pond with 3 courses of bricks. Check the horizontal level with the spirit level. Clean the wall with the edge of the trowel so that it is free from sharp bits of mortar.

6 Locating the deck posts

Establish where the deck posts need to be. For those to the side of the pond dig holes and set them in concrete, and for the ones in the pond make up concrete pads 350 mm square and 150 mm deep. Position on top of an extra layer of geotextile.

7 Finishing the deck frame

Fix the horizontal framework to the posts at the side of the pond so that they are all level with each other. Cut the remaining posts to length, rest them on the concrete pads and bolt them to the horizontals.

8 Haunching with mortar

Ensure that the posts on the concrete pads are haunched with mortar to stop any possible horizontal movement. Trowel the mortar to a smooth finish. Once set, paint the pads with black tanking paint.

9 Fixing the deck boards and completing the pond

Carefully nail on the decking boards using the strip of plywood to set gaps of 6–7 mm and two nails at each junction. Cover the brick wall and exposed edge of the lining with turf or soil and plant grass seed.

Mosaic pond

Ideal for a small garden or courtyard, this elegant circular fountain pond will both cool the air and make the music of water. Its timeless, classical shape will fit in any outdoor room. The mosaic design is a special touch that adds style to your water feature and gives you the opportunity to be creative; if you don't like the fish shapes, look for other images, colours, shapes and patterns that inspire you.

Considering the design

The only limiting factor in this design is the size of the plastic sump. Make sure that you can get one the right size. If you want to keep the mosaic bright, you will need to keep the water sparkling and sterile. Use bromine tablets available from a swimming pool supply company. As always, consider child safety (see page 13).

Getting started

Once you have decided where to site the pond, consider how you are going to get electrical power to it. You are creating a work of art so do not hurry – enjoy it.

Overall dimensions and general notes

← 1.63 m diameter →

403 mm high

Lined with concrete and covered in a bold mosaic design

The pond can be increased in size but it should not be made any smaller, as the joints between the bricks become too wide.

You will need

Materials

- ✔ Wood: 2 pieces 1.74 m x 80 mm x 20 mm, 2 pieces 1.7 m x 80 mm x 20 mm, 4 pieces 702 mm x 80 mm x 20 mm, 2 pieces 540 mm x 80 mm x 20 mm and 2 pieces 500 mm x 80 mm 20 mm (for the formwork), 1 piece 660 mm x 35 mm x 35 mm (tramel arm), 1 piece 150 mm x 70 mm x 70 mm (tramel block)
- ✔ Nails: 36 at 70 mm long
- ✔ Concrete: 1 part cement (100 kg) and 4 parts ballast (400 kg)
- ✔ Plywood: 1 piece 500 mm square x 6 mm thick (trammel base) and 1 piece 1.4 m x 590 mm x 10 mm (concrete former)
- ✔ Bricks: 192

- ✔ Mortar: 1 part cement (50 kg) and 3 parts sand (150 kg)
- ✔ Cobbles: 140 for decorating the wall and 100 kg to fill the sump
- ✔ Rigid plastic sump: 895 mm in diameter (380 mm diameter sump) and 185 mm deep
- ✔ Butyl: 1 piece 2.3 m square
- ✔ Plastic pipe (length to suit your site)
- ✔ Duct tape
- ✔ Thin card: 1 piece 400 mm square
- ✔ Glazed tiles: 30, in an assortment of colours (see page 85)
- ✔ Waterproof tile cement and grout
- ✔ Pump

Tools

- ✔ Tape measure, pegs, string, piece of chalk and a spirit level
- ✔ Club hammer and claw hammer
- ✔ Spade and shovel
- ✔ Wheelbarrow and bucket
- ✔ General-purpose saw and hacksaw
- ✔ Bricklayer's towel and pointing trowel
- ✔ Scissors
- ✔ Brick hammer
- ✔ Jigsaw

Plan view showing foundation formwork and method of laying bricks

Earth

Trammel base
Plywood, 500 mm
square, 6 mm thick

Concrete

600 mm

Trammel arm
660 mm long and
35 mm square.
A 70 mm long nail
projects 20 mm
from end of arm
(so that trammel
scribes a
600 mm radius)

Trammel block
150 mm long
and 70 mm
square. Two
nails, 70 mm
long, are used to
fix block to base)

Trammel pivot
A 70 mm long
nail, positioned
80 mm from
end of arm

Formwork

Trammel base is weighted down by four
bricks and is raised by the height of one
brick after each course is completed

Cut-away plan view (before concrete is applied)

Plastic pipe
To protect
electric cable

Duct tape
To hold pipe in
position while
concrete is applied

Butyl

Sump

Bricks
Soldier
course

Butyl is trapped under
the soldier course

Cross-section showing method of applying concrete

Concrete former
Plywood, 1.4 m x 590 mm x 10 mm
1 grid square = 50 mm

Half of the
coping brick is
cut away to
make room
for the pipe

Concrete rises
38 mm above
the top of the
butyl liner

Plastic pipe
To protect the
electric cable

Coping

Brick wall

Butyl

Sump

Concrete

Use a 100 mm
thick layer of
hardcore under
the concrete if
your soil is loose
and crumbly

Pump

Brick
To raise pump of bottom
and to minimise silt intake

Exploded view of the mosaic pond

Mosaic
A selection of glazed
bathroom tiles

Bricks
Leave a minimum of
8–10 mm wide gaps
between the bricks

Concrete

Plastic sump
895 mm total diameter
380 mm diameter sump
185 mm deep

Butyl

**Concrete
foundation**
80 mm thick

Fixed together
with two 70 mm
long nails at
each junction

500 mm-long

702 mm-long
45° ends

540 mm-long

1.74 m-long

1.7 m-long

Formwork
All pieces of wood are
80 mm x 20 mm in section

Plan view of
the mosaic pattern

1 grid square = 50 mm

Making the mosaic pond

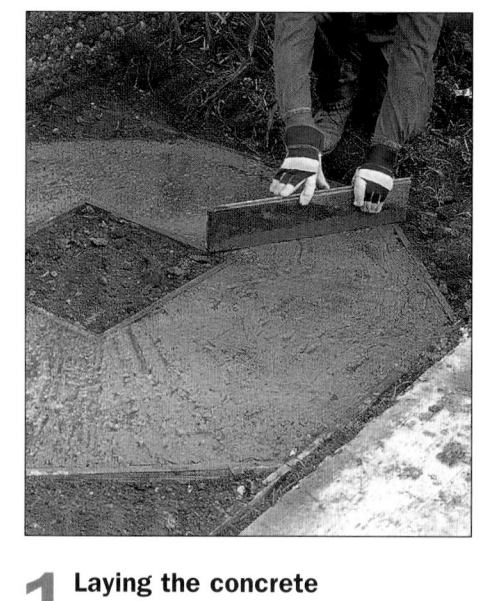

1 Laying the concrete
Cut the 80 mm x 20 mm wood to size and build the formwork. Dig out the foundation to a depth of 200 mm, set the formwork in place and check it is horizontal using the spirit level. Pour in concrete and tamp it level with the top of the frame using an offcut.

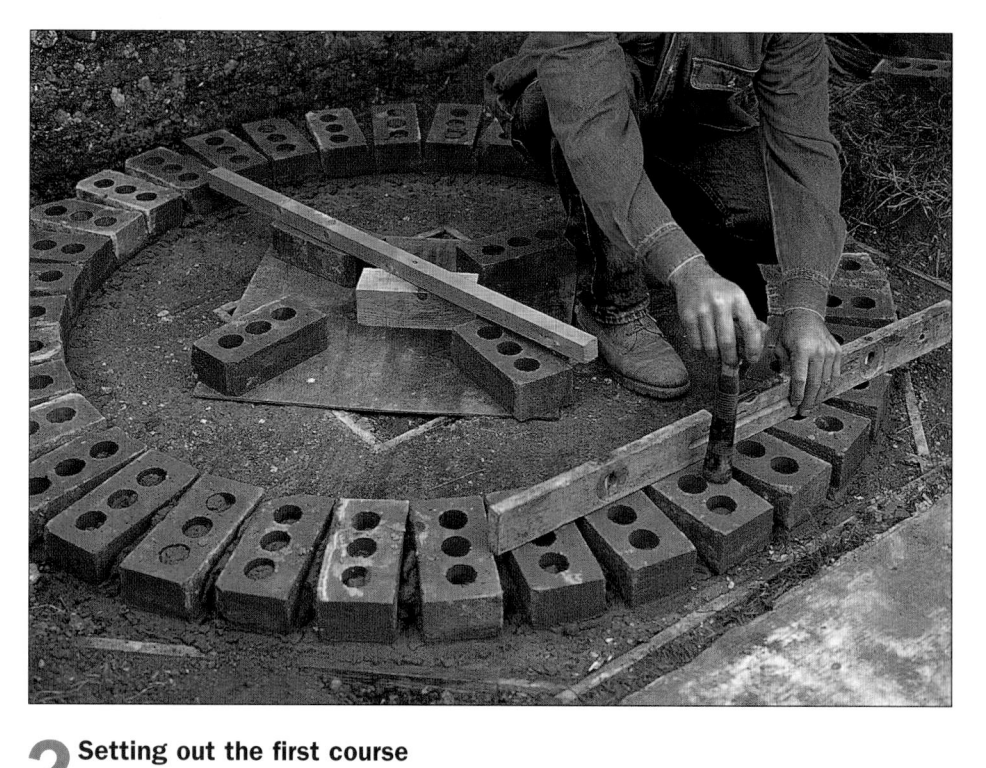

2 Setting out the first course
Build the trammel so that it scribes a 600 mm radius and use this to help you position the bricks. Bed the bricks on mortar, and check them with the spirit level. Build three more staggered courses of brick raising the trammel for each course.

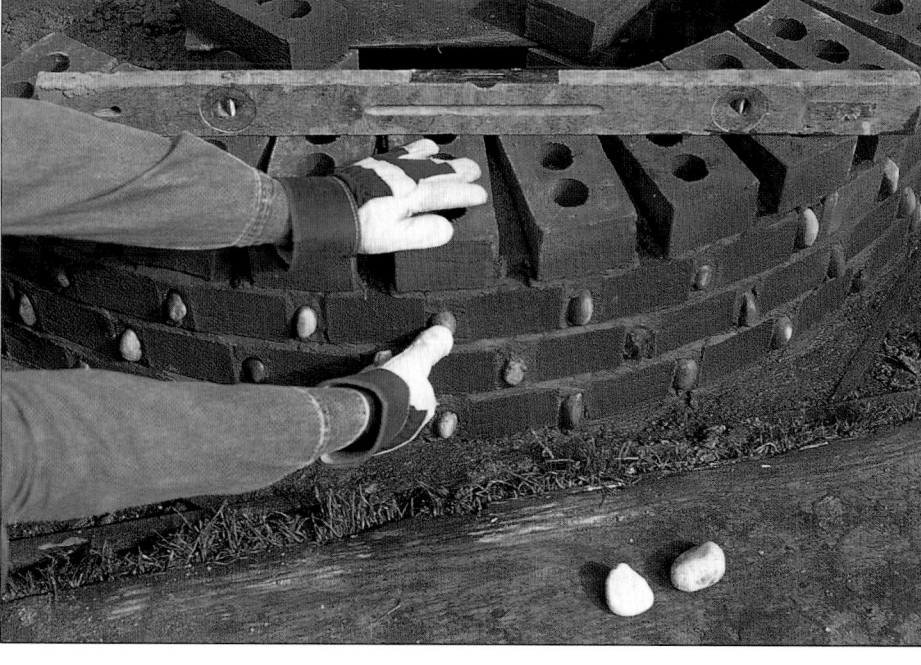

3 Placing the decorative cobbles
Fill each of the angled joints with mortar and decorate with cobbles. Carefully select the cobbles for best effect.

4 Putting in the sump
Dig the earth out from the centre of the foundation slab and set the plastic sump in place to make sure it fits.

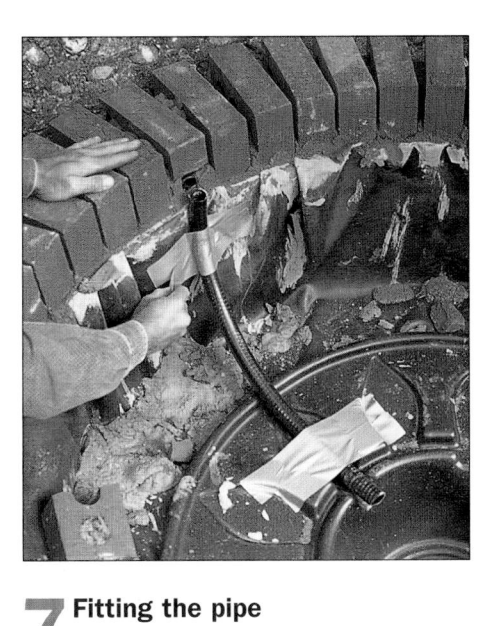

5 Fitting the butyl
Remove the plastic sump, drape the butyl over the whole pond and arrange it so that the folds are evenly distributed. Replace the sump and trim the butyl ensuring you leave a generous overlap on top of the wall.

6 Laying the coping bricks
Lay the top layer of soldier bricks (the coping) around the edge of the pond using the trammel to guide you. Take extra care to space the bricks evenly and check each one is horizontal using the spirit level. Leave out one of the bricks at the back (see step 7).

7 Fitting the pipe
Lay a short length of pipe for taking the electric cable under the last brick of the soldier course (cut the brick in half). Run more pipe from the edge of the sump to the level of the coping bricks and hold it in position with short lengths of duct tape.

8 Tamping the concrete
Use the jigsaw to cut the profile board to shape. Make sure the profile allows for an adequate thickness of concrete as illustrated in the diagram on page 84. Trowel a thick, dry concrete mix inside the pond and use the board to assist in spreading it smoothly.

9 Applying the mosaic
Cut out a fish shape from the card and use this to mark out the design. Break the tiles into small pieces and stick them down. When completed, wipe grout into the gaps and allow to dry. Position the pump in the sump and cover with cobbles.

Split-level pool

★ ★ ★
Advanced

**Making time
5 weekends**
*1 day planning, 4 days
to dig and lay the
foundation and 5 days
to complete*

If you have a sloping or terraced area in your garden it is a good idea to take advantage of the changes in level and build a stream (see page 42) or split-level pools like these. Plan the project so you can see and hear the waterfall while sitting in your favourite spot. The spray from the waterfall will stain the surrounding brickwork and algae will grow on the brick. Over years this will look more and more attractive.

Considering the design

Remember that the water will splash outwards as far as it has fallen, so do not make the bottom pond too small or you will have damp and slippery areas outside the pond as well as lose considerable amounts of water. When you have a waterfall you also get a fair amount of evaporation so you will want to consider an automatic top-up system.

Getting started

There will be a good deal of spoil generated in the excavation of this project, so make sure you have planned where it is to go before you start work.

Overall dimensions and general notes

This split-level design takes a lot of planning but is certainly worth achieving. It is a great way of combining fish, still-water plants and a classic waterfall feature.

Plan the construction so that both ponds finish at ground level

3.665 m long

1.415 m wide

Use an ordinary slab or make a specially shaped tile for lining the spillway

You will need

Materials

- Hardcore: 0.5 cu metres
- Concrete: 1 part cement (750 kg) and 4 parts ballast (3000 kg)
- Blocks: 35
- Bricks: 134 (coping) and 432 (brick spacing and walls)
- Tile: 235 mm x 200 mm x 35 mm (for spillway), can be a flat tile or a specially made ceramic or concrete shape
- Mortar: 1 part cement (150 kg) and 3 parts sand (450 kg)

- Geotextile: 33 sq metres
- Glue: quick drying (for sticking geotextile to wall)
- Duct tape
- Butyl: 1 piece 4 m x 2.6 m and 1 piece 2.3 m x 2.6 m
- Plastic pipe: 1 piece 4 m long (delivery pipe) and 1 piece to protect electric cable (length to suit your site)
- Tanking paint: 16 sq metre coverage
- Pump

Tools

- Tape measure, pegs, string and a piece of chalk
- Spade, fork and shovel
- Spirit level
- Line set
- Brick hammer
- Bricklayer's trowel and pointing trowel
- Scissors
- Hacksaw
- Float
- Paint brush

Cross-section of the split-level pool

Bottom pond
*375 mm lower
than the top pond*

**Double-
thickness walls**
Brick and blocks

Spillway

Top pond

Coping bricks

*Maximum
water height*

Pond lining
*Occurs in cavity
between walls*

Concrete slab
*50 mm thick,
covering liner*

Pump

Brick spacing
*For raising level
during foundation
construction*

Pond lining

Concrete slab
*50 mm thick,
covering liner*

Hardcore
70 mm thick

**Concrete
foundation**
220 mm thick

Plan view of the split-level pool

Pump
*Located on the
bottom of the pond*

Delivery pipe
*Exits bottom
pond here*

Power cable
*Protected by plastic
pipe that exits here*

Top pond
*2.335 m x 985 mm
(inside dimensions)*

Delivery pipe
*Travels length of top
pond and enters here*

Bottom pond
985 mm x 685 mm (inside dimensions)

Spillway
235 mm wide

Floating plants
*Plants that prefer still water will survive
in the top pond (not the bottom pond)*

Exploded view of the split-level pool (lining not shown)

Spillway tile
*235 mm x 200 mm x 35 mm
(for spillway), can be a flat
tile or a specially made
ceramic or concrete shape*

Delivery pipe
*Bricks are cut to accomodate
pipe within the wall cavity.
Pipe exits under the coping bricks
(no holes are made in liner)*

Coping bricks

**Internal wall
to bottom pond**
440 mm high

**Internal wall
to top pond**
440 mm high

**External wall
to top pond**
440 mm high

Power cable and delivery pipes
*Bricks are cut to accomodate
pipes within the wall cavity.
Pipes exit under the coping bricks
(no holes are made in liner)*

**External wall to
bottom pond**
440 mm high

Concrete foundation
2.755 m x 1.677 m x 220 mm

Blocks

Concrete foundation
1.677 m x 1.34 m x 220 mm

Hardcore
70 mm thick

Hardcore
70 mm thick

Brick spacing
*For raising level
during foundation
construction*

Making the split-level pool

1 Excavating
Mark out the area of the foundation slabs for both ponds. Dig down to a depth of 852 mm. Spread hardcore in the bottoms of the holes, compact it to a thickness of 70 mm with a sledgehammer and cast the 220 mm thick concrete slabs.

2 Building the exterior walls
Mark out the size and positions of the exterior walls. Build up the exterior walls to a height of 440 mm using blocks for the first course and bricks for the rest. Clean up all the joints between the bricks that will remain visible.

3 Lining with geotextile
Remove or flatten any sharp objects and carefully line the entire area with geotextile right to the top, folding or cutting away darts formed at the corners, and sticking it to the walls with quick-drying glue. Trim off any geotextile that rises above the top of the walls.

4 Lining with butyl
Position the butyl liner over the geotextile, and use bricks wrapped in geotextile to push the liner into the corners. If necessary refold the creases to make them even and use tape to hold the butyl in place. Trim the liner 100 mm above the top of the bricks.

5 Fitting the pipework
Install a pipe to carry water from the pump in the bottom pond to the far end of the top pond. The second pipe is for the power cable. The pipes do not pierce the liner; they travel up the wall (in the cavity) and over the top (under the coping).

6 Laying more geotextile

Remove the wrapped bricks and reline the hole with a second layer of geotextile as before taking great care not to damage or pierce the butyl. Hang the liner over the top of the butyl at the top of the brickwork.

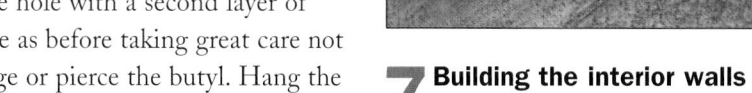

7 Building the interior walls

Use more blocks and bricks to build interior walls allowing for a 10 mm cavity and making a combined wall thickness of 215 mm. Finish at the same height as the exterior wall. You will need to cut blocks and bricks to accomodate the plastic pipes.

8 Fitting the coping bricks

Trim the geotextile level with the top of the walls and trim the butyl again leaving just 50 mm for folding over. Lay the coping bricks around the edge on a bed of mortar. You will need to cut a few bricks to accomodate the plastic pipes.

9 Laying the concrete bottom

Lay a 50 mm thick concrete slab over the liner in the bottom of the pond. After it has set paint the interior of the pond with black tanking paint and allow to dry completely. Fit the tile in the spillway and install the pump. Let everything dry before filling with water.

Acknowledgments

The vision and skill of Rosemary Wilkinson made this book possible. Clare Sayer ably realised and edited the work and, with the help of the Bridgewaters, has produced a work of which we can all be proud.

I found the space between concept and reality something of a curate's egg and could not have persisted without Clare's charming prompts, Jane, David and the support and help of many who shall remain nameless.

Anthony Archer-Wills first inspired me as to the mysteries of water whilst I was at Merrist Wood College, tutored by Paul Colinridge, Tony Begg, Pauline May and Geoff Ace. The demands of workmates, students and clients with the knowledge and pain gained working with Anthony made necessary this primer about ponds.

My gratitude to the above as well as, to name a few: Mr and Mrs A D Allanson, Mr and Mrs J Ashpool, Mr and Mrs D Bradbury, Mrs P Brenan, Mr and Mrs P Corbett, Ms X Coventry, Mr and Mrs H Davies, P G Jeeves, Mr and Mrs I Keith, Mr David Kiff and Berkeley Homes, Mr and Mrs P Graves, Harveys, Hirsts, Lulubelle for inspiration, Mr and Mrs W Matthews, Mr and Mrs G David Neame, Mr and Mrs W Nicholson, Ms Poppy Totman, Robbie and Rosina, Mr and Mrs J Simon, Sonya, Toby Wear, Véronique and the pond makers of England.

I would also like to thank the following people for letting us photograph their ponds: Linda Davis (page 7), Major L Cave (pages 14 and 32), Mrs J Isaacs (page 43), Gillian Harris (page 47), Anne-Marie Bulat/John Brookes (pages 59 and 89), Camilla Hyde (page 65) and Mr and Mrs Shepard Walwyn (page 77).

New Holland Publishers (UK) Ltd would like to thank the following companies for supplying pictures: Forsham Cottage Arks, page 15) and OASE (page 19 bottom right: lights). See Suppliers on page 95 for further details.